Leap
Before
You
Look

72 shortcuts for
getting out of your mind
and into the moment

Arjuna Ardagh

Sounds True, Inc., Boulder CO 80306

© 2008 Arjuna Ardagh

Published 2008

10 9 8 7 6 5 4 3 2 1

Library of Congress Cataloging-in-Publication Data

Ardagh, Arjuna.
  Leap before you look : 72 shortcuts for getting out of your mind and into the moment /
Arjuna Ardagh.
     p. cm.
  ISBN 978-1-59179-636-7 (softcover)
  1. Spiritual life. I. Title.

BL624.A715 2008
204'.4--dc22

2008000575

Book design by Dean Olson

Printed in Canada

⊕ This book is printed on recycled paper containing 100% post-consumer waste and processed without chlorine.

Leap Before You Look

Also by Arjuna Ardagh

Awakening into Oneness
Let Yourself Go
The Translucent Revolution
The Last Laugh
How About Now
Relaxing into Clear Seeing
Living Essence Audio Series
Living Essence Live (Audio)

For Chameli, my partner in Translucent Practice,
and Abhi and Shuba, my sons and teachers

Contents

Contents

Introduction

....

MEET FRED.

From a very early age, Fred had felt that something was missing in his life. Quite early on, after reading the right books and listening to the right teachers, he came to understand what was wrong: he had lost his cello. So, as a young man, Fred became a cello seeker.

Every now and then he'd hear cello music—far off, just a hint, but enough to remember: the purpose of his life was to find his missing cello. He toured the world, and wherever he heard cello music, or even just the word "cello" whispered on the wind, he would follow. Fred climbed the highest mountains, dove into the deepest oceans, trudged across the farthest deserts, all in search of his cello. He met many great teachers and tutors, visited countless concert halls and music schools, and sought out the finest quartets, quintets, and orchestras. He joined support groups, where people would gather in circles to rediscover their inner cello. He bought books and videos with titles like *Ten Steps to Cello Discovery*. Over and over he asked, "Can you help me find my very own cello?" He was passionate, dedicated, and intense. Fred was a full-time professional cello seeker.

One day, after many decades of living a life where everything else had become secondary to his quest, he was rushing down the street to a cello seekers' support group meeting. He was looking only at the pavement, focused on where he needed to go, when he collided with an old friend.

"Fred, where are you going in such a hurry?" asked the friend.

"I don't have time to talk to you now," Fred retorted. "I'm on my way to my cello finders' support group meeting. I can't stop."

But Fred's friend caught his arm, and held him there on the street. "Just wait a minute, Fred. Hold on. What is that thing on your back?"

"What's what on my back?" asked Fred.

"That big, wooden, curvy, stringy, hollow, strange-shaped thing?"

Fred glanced impatiently over his shoulder. "I don't have time to bother with unidentified, wooden, curvy, stringy things. Time is short. I have to find my cello."

"But that thing on your back, that ain't no trombone, fella. And that sure ain't no violin or saxophone either. You'd better take a look."

Finally, just to get rid of this interference so he could carry on with his search, Fred agreed to look over his shoulder, to stop, to pay attention. To his shock and amazement, Fred discovered that strapped onto his back was a large cello. He was flabbergasted. He didn't know what to say. He sat down—right there on the sidewalk. He took the cello onto his lap, tears streaming down his face. Fred laughed and laughed and laughed. He had finally found what he had always been looking for.

With trembling hands, he took the bow and rosined it. Holding it in one hand and the cello in the other, he fell absolutely silent and still. His eyes glazed over, as though he were staring at an object on the other side of the universe. He rested deeply in a state of absolute cello reunion, of oneness with the cello.

"What's with you, Fred?" his friends and family asked.

"The search is over, that's what's with me. I've found my cello. I am free of my search. I have realized my essential cello-carrying nature." Fred looked at people with long and meaningful stares. Children would run away. But Fred just went on sitting there, cello in one hand, bow in the other, staring and silent.

And that, dear friends, is the end of the story.

Or is it? From the perspective of being a cello seeker, of having always been a cello seeker, that's it. Within the story of Fred's whole life being about rediscovering something lost, that *could* be the end of the story. We leave Fred sitting silently and contentedly with his cello, and nothing ever happens again.

From another point of view, however, much more is possible for Fred, now that he is reunited with his cello. His story could have many more chapters—chapters about *music*. Fred could bring the bow to the cello and begin to play; he could find out what is possible when he not only enjoys his discovery but lives it, makes it into art, and gives it as a gift to all of humanity.

Now, if Fred begins to play the cello, the music he creates may not be so beautiful right away. I happen to know this from firsthand experience, because my wife has been learning the cello. When someone first starts to play the cello, it can sound a little like a cat being skinned alive. But the more you play the cello, the more beautiful it becomes. With regular practice, your playing becomes the expression of a great beauty that was previously latent. Transforming the discovery of a cello into the gift of bringing music to the world requires regular practice.

Anyone who plays a musical instrument knows the importance of practice. We all know the story about the man who, upon arriving at New York's Grand Central Station, stopped a passerby and asked, "Excuse me, how do I get to Carnegie Hall?" "Practice, practice, practice," was the reply.

This is a book about practice.

Practice is the bridge between your unmanifest potential and your manifest capacity to give. You practice not to reach a goal, but to create beauty. You practice not for the future, but for a more ecstatic now. If you play music, if you paint, if you write poetry, you know that there is no end to the expression of that beauty. It would be absurd to suggest so, wouldn't it? Can you imagine that you might play an instrument for decades and then one day come to a point where you just played the perfect note? "Good, well that's done. Now I can give up the cello and take up golf instead." That would be ridiculous, wouldn't it? We all know that whatever our art form, be it building houses, gardening, writing, or raising children, the possibility of gifting is endless.

....

In recent years, many people just like you have fallen into a realization even more pivotal than Fred's. They have fallen into the realization of who they are deeper than the mind, a realization of *being* silence, of *being* peace, of *being* infinity. Such a realization may come in short snapshots or in more abiding resting, but either way it changes everything. People from all walks of life are coming to the discovery that what they have been seeking outside themselves is actually who they are, and who they were all along. What they have been seeking is in fact the medium, the stillness, in which everything else arises. They see that who they are is the silence in which sound is happening, the spaciousness in which movement occurs. This kind of recognition, whether fleeting or abiding, is called an awakening.

It might happen when you are out hiking and you notice the expansiveness of the view, reminding you in that moment of the expansiveness of your own true nature. It could happen after many years of meditation and watching the activity of mind, when suddenly in an "aha!" moment there is the recognition of that which is watching the mind—silence itself—and that it is beyond and untouched by the mind. It might happen while dancing, or playing a musical instrument, or making love. Suddenly, you find that there is only the lovemaking—no commentary, no evaluation, no thought at all. In such moments, everything resolves itself. You are completely now, completely here. The activity of mind may continue, but it recedes, becoming as remote as the sounds of the TV from a neighbor's apartment, leaving just the perfection of this moment.

Many of us carry elaborate theories about spiritual states, concepts we have read or heard and borrowed, which we tend to put above our own experience. As a result, we often overlook the simplicity of what is already here. Since 1991, I have been teaching weekend seminars all over the world that point people back to the simple mystery of who they are, in this moment, deeper than the activity of the mind. Many of them come to these seminars with ideas about being incomplete, of something missing. In paying attention to what is already here, in this moment, it's not that what was missing is given to them, but that what was already there is recognized.

Just as for Fred, when he discovered that his cello was on his back all along, a moment of awakening, or even a more abiding realization, may seem to be the end. "For years and years and years I've been seeking. My whole identity has been that of a spiritual seeker. And now in this recognition, there's nothing to do. All is perfect. I'm just going to sit here under this tree and watch the grass grow." But this is only the end of a story relative to being a seeker.

Relative to the ungiven gifts in your heart, relative to why your body took birth at all, it is the beginning: the beginning of a life of meaning, of purpose, of integrity, of music. We discover that who you are, who I am, who everyone is, is less of an entity and more of a presence. Not even *a* presence, but *presence itself*, with no boundaries, no beginning or end in time. That living presence is empty of form and content, but full of love, full of creative intelligence. Presence is that which is aware of all that is changing. In order for the recognition of that latent presence—that silence beneath the noise—to be transformed into a gift and a blessing, practice is needed.

By some estimates, millions of people are coming into this kind of realization today, perhaps just in glimpses, but enough to radically change their relationship to themselves, to reality, and to spiritual life and practice. They are no longer seeking, exactly, because the secret has been revealed. Their interest shifts to the deepening and embodiment of the realization.

There are multiple theories available about why this is happening today to so many people, which I have explored in great depth in my previous books. But this book is not about why, it is about *how*. This book will offer you a variety of simple tools, most of which take just a few minutes, to both precipitate the shift out of the mind and into awakening, and to deepen and embody that awakening in ordinary day-to-day life.

This book explores the possibility of spiritual practice not as a means to a goal but as an endlessly unfolding exploration of a life of beauty—a life worth living.

A Life of Paradox

When we are willing to exchange our life of preoccupation with "me" and "my needs" for a life given in the service of love itself, of that presence itself, we are faced with an interesting paradox.

On one side of the paradox, we recognize that everything is perfect just as it is. When the chatter of the mind recedes just a little bit, when the smells, colors, and textures of the world become more immediately felt, we recognize the grace running through it all. Even in conflict, or in the midst of what we call suffering, if we are really in touch with the pulse of life itself, we can feel the beauty of it all.

On the other side of the paradox, we realize that everything is continuously evolving. Our human condition, as it is now, is flawed with unconscious habits, addictions, and compulsions. In seeing the gap between who we are today and who we could be, seeing the trickle of gifting that's coming through us relative to the latent torrent that we intuit, we bow in humility. When we look down from our resting point on the mountain, we may marvel at how far we have come from the valley below, but when we look up, the peaks are still lofty and daunting, and we know there is still much more to discover.

Between these two poles of paradox, that everything is perfect as it is on one side and everything is evolving and imperfect on the other side, lies the art of translucent spiritual practice—the art of practice with no goal. I borrowed the word "translucent," usually used to describe the physical universe, in my 2005 book *The Translucent Revolution*. Translucence describes a medium that is neither opaque nor transparent. A wall, for example, is completely opaque—light cannot pass through it. A sheet of glass, if it's really clean, is transparent—you could walk right up to it and bang your nose, because you might not even see that it's there. A translucent medium, on the other hand, is neither opaque nor transparent: a sheet of frosted glass, a colored crystal, or a sculpture made of colored glass. Translucent objects maintain their form, color, and texture, yet they allow light to pass through them. When you shine light on a translucent object, it appears to glow from within. Translucent people are neither opaque nor transparent. They are no longer glued to their own separate agenda and allegiance to beliefs held in the mind, and in that sense they are not opaque. But they also have the honesty and humility to recognize that the habits of the personality remain, and could never perfectly reflect presence. They are lit up by their deepest nature, yet they remain fully engaged in their daily personal lives. Translucent people also appear to glow as if from within themselves.

Any kind of translucent practice, like the many invitations in this book, will allow you to be lit up by a radical awakening to who you really are, to be lit up by an awakening to the silence underneath the noise, the spaciousness underneath the movement. But you will also retain the humility, the sanity, and the honesty to face your human condition, just as it is, and to allow this human monkey to be nothing more than that, a monkey without much hair.

Translucent spiritual practice walks along the razor's edge. We practice not to attain a future goal but in respect for the sacredness of this very moment. We practice so that whatever has been realized, whatever is the deepest recognition of the heart, can be given as an offering, an expression of gratitude for the beauty of this moment. When we are no longer obsessed with trying to attain something in the future, we are practicing for now, for this moment. All that is left is to make this moment now a more beautiful moment, a work of art rather than a striving for something more.

As we walk this razor's edge, there is always the danger of falling to one side or to the other. If we fall to one side, we fall into self-congratulation, the delusion that our human condition is somehow perfected or enlightened. Then we become unwilling to face our humanity and be honest about what we find. We want to grab on to the perch of lofty spiritual states with both our taloned feet, and can't wait to tell our friends just how impressed we are with ourselves. I'm sure you've met people who've become obsessed with their own attainment. Maybe at some point you have even met someone like that when you've looked in the mirror; I know that I have. When we fall to that side of the edge, evolution stops, because we are no longer willing to look, be honest, and feel. We cling to the thought: *I am enlightened. I have made it. I have got it. I've had the insight, haven't you?* Not only does evolution stop, but so do most of our friendships.

On the other hand, we can also fall to the other side of the razor's edge, into the endless treadmill of self-improvement. There, we become fixated on all of the things that are still wrong with us, all of the things that need to be fixed. Then, we start to worry. "Maybe the reason that I'm not more open and loving and accepting is because of that thing that happened with my mother when I was four. I'd better go back to my therapist and work on that some more. And maybe that's not enough? Maybe I also need to involve the body and perhaps release tension from the solar plexus." We start to worry that perhaps the way we are eating or exercising is not correct. We try to manifest all kinds of things and qualities to make life conform to our ideas of how it should be. Our attempts to make this poor human monkey into an improved human monkey become endless. In our obsession with self-improvement, we are so busy focusing on what could be that we overlook the perfection of now. We become so busy with how we could be better that we no longer smell the scent of the evening jasmine. We no longer feel the mystery behind the eyes of our beloved. We no longer taste the food we eat. Everything becomes about tomorrow: "When I've finally fixed myself, then I can live."

Of course, we will inevitably fall from the razor's edge again and again. From time to time, all of us slip into marveling at our attainment or into convincing ourselves that we must fix everything before we can really enjoy life. But there's a beauty once we see this process, once we recognize the paradox itself. A translucent life is self-regulating. When we stray too far into self-congratulation, something begins to dry up, like a plant that's no longer receiving water. We can talk about the presence, but it is no longer living us, as a shimmering mystery. Life becomes repetitive, a reenactment of the same state over and over again. As soon as we start cherishing ourselves, the very richness of the realization that brought us to do so disappears.

Similarly, if we stray too far into self-improvement and get too busy, something deep within us calls out for that perfume of the divine, the knowing that everything is blessed in this moment.

Something within us intuitively knows that there is no need to work for what is already here, and demands that we snap our fingers and be free.

And so it is that we stray and return and stray and return to the middle way, where everything is perfect and imperfect in the same breath.

Recycling What Is Old

Right down the middle lies the art of translucent spiritual practice, where we simultaneously feel the perfection of this moment and at the same time recognize the endless possibilities for improving our human condition. To live in a way that embraces this paradox cannot be done in the mind, because they are mutually exclusive. You can't *understand* your way into this, you can only live it as an art form. Then, in each moment of this love affair with love itself, each moment at the feet of the imminence of what can be given, we use all that is available. We use the broken, absurd, and somewhat dysfunctional habits of the personality to make art. We use all that we've got, all the habits of this separate individual, in the service of something much deeper—the heart's deepest recognition.

Where I live, in Nevada County, California, there is a recycling yard where you are invited to bring all the things you no longer need. They are separated into metal, plastic, and paper, and reused for other purposes. This recycling yard is set in a very beautiful rural valley surrounded by rolling hills. Although it's full of broken stuff, it has a unique charm. At the entrance of the recycling yard, someone has created a magnificent sculpture of a man panning for gold; this was once a gold mining area. The entire statue, all thirty feet of it, has been made from things that people brought to the recycling yard. If you look, you can see the rims from car wheels, bits of a dishwasher, pieces of drainpipe from the side of a building. You can see all kinds of things that no longer serve their original purpose but here have been transformed into art. I can't imagine how many people drive every day to dump their recycling and are somehow transformed, amused, or inspired by this work of art.

In the same way, translucent spiritual practice takes the habits of the personality, the habits of desire and fear and addiction that once served the obsession with a separate *me*, and uses them to serve a higher value. Now, they serve love itself; they serve the divine presence as art. We enter into translucent practice not to get somewhere else, not to achieve a goal, but in a deep love affair with this moment.

When I was researching my book *The Translucent Revolution*, I had a long phone conversation with my friend Lama Surya Das, the first Western-born lama in the Tibetan Buddhist tradition. The depth of Lama Surya's awakening is astounding. When you connect with him, you know that there's clearly no doubt left in him that his true nature is limitless consciousness, that his true nature is silence, even though thoughts continue within the silence. He is, you could say, a truly awakened man, and yet he continues every day to do quite intricate spiritual practices from the Tibetan tradition, and other traditions as well. He spends many hours a day in sitting meditation, in chanting, in different postures.

"Surya," I said to him, "obviously the seeking is completed for you. It seems that you know the truth of your real nature. So, why do you practice? Is it because you want to deepen the realization, to come to some deeper, further state of awakening?" "I don't know," he said. "I have no choice. This is just who I am. It's what I love. Some people love to play tennis. Some people love to play the flute. I love this. I love sitting. I love chanting. I love practice."

Lama Surya Das involves himself in spiritual practice not as work to get somewhere, but as an art form.

Not My Thoughts

Until there is some kind of awakening, some kind of a recognition of presence or grace, our relationship to the habits of personality will always be one of resistance and modification. This means that as long as we overlook the grace underlying all things, we only know the things themselves. When anger arises, we only know the anger. When fear is there, we only know the fear. Thus, everything that arises is met with a commentary of should and shouldn't.

When all one knows are feelings and thoughts and events that are constantly changing, then the only approach available is to struggle with them, to try to make things better. This means that we try to resist things as they are, or modify them, or even cling to some things and try to make them more; but because things are always changing, there is no resolution, no peace. It is rather like watching TV, but forgetting that it is TV. All you know is changing the channel. As soon as you remember that you are watching TV, something else becomes available, which is to relax more deeply into the sofa, and into the recognition that although you are watching TV, you are not contained within the world of the TV. Self-improvement is only about changing content, and our internal reactions to that content; awakening is about liberation from the dimension of changing content. Only when you awaken to *being* that deeper presence does an alternative become available.

In the willingness to live the paradox, and to let the paradox live us, we develop a very different relationship to the habits of the personality. As soon as there is some kind of dropping in, even for a moment, to a recognition of the deeper dimension of things, things start to shift. This is true for so many people today. Then, we can recognize the sky as well as the clouds, the ocean as well as the boats, and thoughts, beliefs, and feelings begin to become experiences we are having rather than who we are. We can recognize anger arising and experience it and watch it moving. We can recognize that even deeply held beliefs are not, strictly speaking, "my" thoughts. The feelings that arise are not exactly "my" feelings. The more deeply we realize who or what we really are, the more we realize that these thoughts have a life of their own. These feelings have an independent existence—they're simply moving through us. They are thoughts without a thinker, feelings without a separate identity to own them.

The more we investigate who is really here, who is really hearing the sounds and seeing the movement, the more we can experience thoughts and feelings as events. Only then do we realize that all of these thoughts and feelings belong to the ancient mind. They belong to the collective mind. My sorrow is your sorrow is our sorrow. My ambition is your ambition is our ambition. As this continues to deepen and the identification with these things loosens, they do not necessarily change, but our relationship to them is transformed from one of resistance to one of enjoyment. One of the greatest miracles of a translucent life is the discovery that absolutely anything can be enjoyed when it is celebrated. Anything can be enjoyed when we make friends with it.

Most of the practices in this book are not aimed at making you a better person, but assisting you in declutching the identification with the habits of the personality. Rather than trying to fix ourselves, here is an invitation to transform yourself, just as you are, into a work of art.

The Return of the Goddess

In a moment of radical awakening, in a moment of the attention turning back to who we are, rather than being obsessed with what we do and how we appear, there is the immediate finger-snap recognition of Oneness, of the limitless ocean of consciousness, the spaciousness and silence of our true nature. That which is realized in a moment of radical awakening has no gender. The sky is neither masculine nor feminine. Silence is neither gender. That presence itself requires no practice. It is. It only requires recognition. It's not something that we attain, but something that we realize has always been there.

The embodiment of realization *does* require practice, just like a musical instrument. It requires that the channels of gifting be continuously opened, more and more freely. As soon as that realization comes down into the body and begins to give itself as a gift to life, the embodiment itself has gender. In fact, it has a unique blueprint, a unique kind of gift, different from any other gift. Awakening lived through an Indian embodiment will be different than through an American embodiment; it will be different in an educated and cultured embodiment than through a simple and uneducated embodiment. And, above all, the embodiment and expression of awakening will be different through a masculine embodiment or a feminine one.

For as long as we have known, spiritual life has been dominated by the masculine. We may think we know what spirituality is, but actually what we know is only the masculine embodiment of awakening. Every major religion in the world was founded by a man, and has been propagated by men. We have little notion of what the feminine embodiment of the awakened heart is like, although it exists in tiny pockets here and there.

Masculine energy is marked by a spirit of breaking through obstacles and reaching goals. When dominated by the masculine, spirituality is concerned with eliminating thoughts from the mind, freeing ourselves of feelings, particularly negative ones, with the goal of breaking through to a state of cosmic void. The term "enlightenment," as it is commonly understood, is a hypermasculine term referring to a complete transcendence of the human condition, the achievement of a set goal after which nothing else needs to happen. The buzzer sounds, and the game is over.

The feminine in all of us, on the other hand, has different interests. The feminine feels the divine when she is able to feel anything fully. Through feeling anything without restriction, be it pain, grief, or anger, she feels God. The feminine in all of us loves texture, music, taste. The feminine in all of us doesn't try to transcend the body, but delights in it and recognizes the body itself as a temple of the divine.

Translucent spiritual practice is characterized by a reemergence of the feminine in spirituality, a reemergence of the Goddess. This is not to say that the Goddess must dominate—that's not the nature of the feminine—but that there can be a reunion of masculine and feminine energy. Spiritual life can be a balance of the masculine: recognizing evolution and movement, continuously setting new goals in its quest for deeper and more, and the feminine: which is in love with this moment, which can feel, touch, and be touched.

When my wife, Chameli, and I take a walk, my job is to look a hundred feet ahead of us. "Let's reach that peak, because that will give us a magnificent view of the valley below." I'm always motivating us to go a little farther. Her job is to point out what I would otherwise miss. "Look at the flowers. Can you smell that bush? Hear the sound of the birds." When we walk together, hand in hand, we are moving forward, but always savoring this moment. Together we enjoy a spiritual practice that is both evolutionary and eternally wedded to the now.

Tailor-Made

Translucent spiritual practice is made to measure. It's not off the rack. The kinds of spiritual practice many of us are used to adhere to a one-size-fits-all principle: if we have a commonly recognized goal of enlightenment, where everyone's going to reach the same goal, and we've defined what that should look like, then everybody can do the same practice. For example, some schools advocate that everybody should chant a mantra. It doesn't matter what's going on. Not enough money? Chant the mantra. Having health problems? Chant the mantra. Ants in the basement? Chant the mantra. This is a one-size-fits-all practice. There are many practices like that, where no matter your disposition, no matter what obstacles you face, the same practice is prescribed as a panacea.

Translucent practice, on the other hand, arises anew for each individual. Everyone needs their own unique balance of practice to bring forth the gifts that are hidden in their unique embodiment. Very often, we are not the best people to choose our own practices, because we tend to choose from our own imbalance. A shy, quiet person will tend to choose a passive meditation, which, of course, only furthers the imbalance. An outgoing, extroverted party animal will choose dancing or drumming as a practice, and avoid meditation.

There are many, many kinds of translucent practice. The best way to decide which practice will suit you best is to consult with your friends—those who know you well. It's often those closest to us—friends, family, mentors, or others who love us—who will be able to see most clearly where there can be room for more art, for more humor.

Often, we can make practice out of that which has seemed to be the biggest problem. Several years ago, a man who was quite an austere, disciplined spiritual practitioner came to a retreat I was leading. Every day, he got up very early in the morning to do long sittings of meditation, yoga, and breath control; he carefully monitored his diet; and he always made sure to get just the right kind of exercise. Despite this impressive regimen, he came to see me with his head hung low in shame. "I really am committed to my path. But the trouble is that in my meditation I often feel drowsy," he said. He even told me, with great shame and in a whisper, "I sometimes fall asleep." I suggested a different kind of practice to him. I suggested that during the retreat, whenever he noticed just the faintest whiff of drowsiness entering his consciousness, that he should right away find the nearest bed and take a nap. I suggested to him that for the course of this retreat, naps should be his primary practice. This was a complete anathema to his habit of thinking. I was suggesting that what had been his greatest impediment should become his practice itself. But I gave one caveat: "When you take a nap, really be there. Really enjoy it. Lie down and closely observe what happens as the body drops into deeper states of relaxation. Really pay attention to the finer points of nap-taking." By the end of the retreat, he told me that he had entered into deeper states of dissolving, surrender, and silence than he ever had through his meditation. What he had previously most avoided as an obstacle became the most potent portal into presence.

Dedicate Your Practice

For most of us, our exploration of a translucent life may well start from "my" needs. We may begin our practice in the hopes of reme-dying deficiencies and imbalances in what we call "me." But sooner or later, the dedication and the motivation of our practice will shift naturally from the "me" to love itself, to life itself. We may start contracted down into an interest in my car, my money, my sex life, my relationship, and then my enlightenment, my spiritual prac-tice. It is all in the interest of the same "me." But ultimately, all real translucent practice leads us to service, our attention shifting from caring just for the little me to being dedicated to the big Me, to the Oneness that includes all sentient beings.

Why should it be that all practice that begins with me ends up in service to the whole? First, it is because the practice itself is con-tinuously helping us see through the myth of a separate identify.

That is what awakening means; that is what oneness means: to see through the obsession with the separate self and to open into the all-inclusive ocean of consciousness. But also, the opening of "me-based" practice into service is actually the only way to fully mature beyond our obsession with separation. As long as we are focused on *my* enlightenment, *my* practice, *my* translucent life, the "my" itself will obstruct the true longing of the heart.

All practice, all spiritual inquiry, all spiritual life begins with me and ends with us. We live together in a very unusual time, a time for which we do not see a precedent in recorded history. We live with a feeling of impending crisis. Peak oil, environmental devastation, terrorism, wars, enormous economic disparity, all of these things tempt us to abandon hope. Many of us have realized that we cannot rely on politicians, intellectual theorists, or even political or environmental activists. If we could rely on these people, then we would be out of the mess already.

In a very real way, it's up to you and me, and to your friends and my friends. It is up to whoever is not completely asleep but is beginning, just beginning, to intuit the true nature of things, to make a change. It's up to you and me not just to enjoy realization but to embody it, to make our lives a practice with no goal, a practice continuously dedicated to the living of the big love.

There is an old adage I grew up with, which says: "Look before you leap." It means think things through; don't act impulsively. Act carefully and with reservation. Dear friend, I think today's world requires of us just the opposite. Before you have time to think things through, before you have time to measure the appropriateness or the prudence of how you live, let your love slip out more quickly than reservation can capture it. Don't look before you leap, but leap before you look. Leap out of the mind into a life of unbridled generosity of spirit. Leap out of habit into the spontaneous flow of real love.

How to Use This Book

....

THERE ARE MANY WAYS TO use the practices in this book. One approach is to first read the book cover-to-cover, to get a feeling for the full scope of the practices, and then return to the practices to which you feel most drawn. Experiment with integrating them into your day. See if, with time, they become natural and automatic.

Second, you could dip into the book anywhere, find a practice with a title that attracts you, and try it out. When you have a sense of mastery with one practice, you can move on to another.

Third, you could familiarize yourself with the practices in the book, learn them one by one, and use them as antidotes in your day-to-day life when old habits and limitations kick in.

But it is through the fourth and final way to use this book that you will squeeze the most juice out of it. Use this book together with a friend, or a community of friends, and instead of selecting your own practice, ask your friends to choose the practices they feel would most help you. If you agree to go through with their suggestions, they will support you and encourage you through the inevitable valleys of doubt or lethargy. Your friends and community then become your teachers.

The practices are organized according to the areas of life that they affect:

- Meditation practices, practiced alone, are designed to calm oneself in order to see oneself and all of life more clearly. Meditation practices are a foundation for the rest of the book.
- Insight practices involve using intelligence and common sense to break through the false beliefs of the mind.
- Daily-routine practices are designed to disrupt the tedium of daily life, bringing a quality of zest and aliveness to those activities that have become automatic.
- Body practices use the physical form to bring us back into the present moment. The body lives perpetually in now; only the mind runs backward and forward in time.
- Feeling practices allow us to transform our relationship to our emotions. Rather than drowning in them, we learn to surf emotions like waves.
- Intimate relationship practices use our connection with other people to open the heart and fill us with wonder and depth of feeling.
- Sex practices, to be used with one's intimate partner, transform sex from desire and addiction into an overflow of giving and worship.
- Family practices allow us to come together as a family and connect deeply with each other in a playful way that all generations can enjoy.
- Nature practices make use of the enormous power of the earth and its countless ways to soothe us and awaken us back into sanity.
- Devotional practices allow us to fall into worship and devotion; when the heart is fully open to anyone or even everyone, the veil of separation lifts.
- Compassion practices help us feel the pain of another as our own pain, the triumphs and defeats of every being as our own condition.

- Community practices bring our spiritual life into social and political action, so that we can make a difference to those around us and our world.

Each practice is rated according to its level of difficulty:
* One star means accessible to anyone, with no experience or preparation necessary.
/* Two or three stars require a little more courage and confidence.
****/***** Four or five stars are more advanced and should be left for those times when you feel like a bigger stretch. They are the bungee jumps of spiritual expansion.

At first, many of the practices may not seem meditative or associated with a spiritual life. How can acting like an idiot in a supermarket possibly bring us closer to God? Read on.

Section One

Meditation Practices

MEDITATION MAY SEEM LIKE SOMETHING you learn, or an activity to do on a regular basis. There are many styles of meditation available today that you can learn from a teacher, on a retreat, or even from a book or a CD. Practicing one style of meditation on a daily basis is without doubt a good idea: it will cultivate presence, watching, inner calm, and peace in the midst of chaos.

But meditation is not only a technique that you learn; it is also a disposition, a way of being with yourself and with life, which you can return to at any time. The Sanskrit word for meditation, "dhyana" (the root of the Japanese word "zen") refers less to a kind of activity than to a state of awareness. It may start with a calming of the usual activities of thought, but it also goes deeper. As the clutch of conceptual thinking loosens, we are able to see things as they are with greater clarity. We can meet reality nakedly, and recognize what is real and what is only imagination. Finally, both experience and experiencer merge into Oneness.

Awakening is sometimes referred to as single moment out of time, and sometimes as a gradual process. The six practices in this section will allow you to know awakening to be both. Any moment in your day can become the diving board into an ocean of living presence that was always there, just beneath the surface of the waves of your life. And, at the same time, the more we return to seeing that ocean, the more it reveals its infinity, in a process that is endless.

These practices can build upon whatever daily practice you may already have, or they may also act as fresh catalysts. Remember that meditation can happen any time; it is a dropping into yourself, and into reality as it is.

1

Expand Peripheral Vision

LEVEL OF DIFFICULTY *

In the midst of your busy day, stop.
Sit quietly with your eyes open.
Look at any object before you.
Now take an in-breath and expand your vision
To include what is immediately to the left and to the right of
that object.
With the out-breath, relax and settle into yourself.
Take another in-breath and expand your vision even more
To include everything that's before you, in an arc of about
ninety degrees.
Breathe out and settle further into yourself.
Take another in-breath and include your entire field of vision.
Your attention is equally distributed between what is
in front of you
And all of your peripheral vision.
Expand it even more to include things not just to the left and
the right,
But even things over your shoulders.
Expand beyond what your eyes can see.
With the out-breath, relax completely into being that which
sees all.
Remain like this, breathing softly, for several minutes.
Feel the mystery of your own essence.

....

Attention can take many states. It can be focused, alert, and single-pointed. Often we need to be like that, like a cat watching a mouse or a bird, ready to pounce. If you drive in traffic, juggle a busy schedule, perhaps while raising children or just working in today's commercial world, you are probably constantly attending to beeping machines, deadlines, and needs from a variety of directions, which sometimes seem impossible to fulfill at the same time. You need to stay focused to get it all done, and there's no time to space out.

This is our habitual state, ready for action, muscles and sinews taught, anticipating the need to make a move. When your attention is focused in this way, you become more defined, a human-doing instrument more than a human-being presence.

Attention can also be more diffused, spread equally over the range of our sensory perception. Then, everything can relax—body, thoughts, and feelings—and we become more of a presence. Now you can feel the forest rather than just busily counting the trees as you hurry through them on your way toward the future.

Because our habits of focus are so familiar, we may think that a more diffused state of consciousness is out of reach. We ascribe it to other people, a teacher, the author of a spiritual book, or even a historical figure, but never to ourselves. We may also project more expansive consciousness into our own future, saying to ourselves, "When I am enlightened, then it will all be different."

But there is no need to make this choice. You can shift to a more expansive view at any time, for a few minutes, and then return to the habits of daily life. Try using this practice often throughout the day.

2

Stop

LEVEL OF DIFFICULTY *

In the midst of your busy day, when there seem to be so many
things to do,
Stop.
Stop moving, stop talking,
Stop what you are doing, and feel.
Hold your body in the same position.
Feel this moment just as it is. Hear the sounds.
Notice the sensations in the body.
Notice the speed and texture of your thoughts.
Remain like this for sixty seconds.
See? The world around you continues, even without your
involvement.
Who are you now, outside of the game?
Now continue with your day.

. . . .

It is easy to make a big deal out of awakened states of consciousness.
They must be the fruit of long years of practice, or the domain of a few
spiritual masters. In fact, if you are really interested in living an awakened life, then what you are longing for is already here, just one flight
down from the usual routine of daily tasks. There is no need to become
anything, or change anything, or heal anything. Just stop and notice
the screen on which the flickering images are being projected, notice
the luminosity that is projecting them. That is who you truly are.

The mind is constantly rushing backward and forward in time: it is busy with desires, fears, and deadlines. Like a computer that can never be switched off, the mind endlessly tries to make reality bow to its agenda. When the mind machine is behind the wheel of our day-to-day life, then everything is about getting somewhere else, somewhere other than where we already are. There is no way out of the machine from within its own activity. The mind can never bring us to presence: it simply makes being in the present moment into a concept about the future. "Later, when I am enlightened, then I will be fully here."

The doorway to sanity is always in this very moment, right here, right now. If you stop what you are doing and become present, the whole energy changes. The momentum of the thought machine is suddenly broken, and you are just here, with things as they are. This simple practice disrupts the patterns of the mind just long enough to remember the sweetness of things as they already are. Use this practice several times a day until it becomes habitual.

3

Pure Waiting

LEVEL OF DIFFICULTY **

Whenever you can, sit and wait.
There is no need to distract yourself by filling the gap with
random activity.
At the gate at the airport,
In the few minutes before it's time to leave the house, while
waiting for the bus,
Rather than picking up a book,
Or flipping the pages of a magazine,
Or checking e-mail or switching on the TV,
Just sit and wait,
Present . . . ready . . . available,
Waiting for the next thing to happen.
No need to meditate or get spiritual.
Just wait, like a cat, or a bird in a tree.
Become the waiting itself.
Wait for the kiss of the divine.
Wait for the kiss that kisses your lips
From the inside.

. . . .

Pure waiting is the supremely meditative state. Usually, we don't
choose it consciously, and we resent it. If we embrace waiting
completely—if we relax into it completely without resistance—the
body can become fully relaxed, while at the same time the senses

become sharp and present. Then, we are available to life, to the divine source.

I have a friend who is a monk. He told me that during his training, the novices were divided into three groups. Those in the first group, like him, were told to go to another area, where each would be given a meditation hut, and to wait there for further instructions. The first day passed, and no one came. Then another day, and another. Food was brought, but no instructions and no instructor. After about a week, from his solitary hut he heard the sounds of someone sweeping the nearby hut that was set aside for the teacher. Surely this meant someone was finally coming! He waited all day, alert, ready, anticipating. But still no one came. After another week, they cleaned the hut again, yet again no one came. By the next week, he realized that the cleaning was simply done on a weekly basis and meant nothing. He and the other novices stayed in their huts like this for three months. During this time, he sometimes felt angry, sometimes bored, sometimes depressed. But through it all, he always remembered that they had told him to sit and wait for further instructions. He told me that his three-month period of waiting was the most important part of his training. In that time, he learned the art of pure waiting. It trained him to listen totally, to be receptive, to be aware without interpretation.

Practice waiting as often as you can, in the simple trust that if you do nothing, sooner or later the perfect thing will happen on its own.

4

Enter the Space Between the Breaths

LEVEL OF DIFFICULTY ***

Become aware of the movement of the breath.

Without trying to change it in any way,

Watch the breath come in.

Just before the in-breath turns into the out-breath, notice the small gap.

Then watch the breath go all the way out.

Just before the in-breath,

There is another small gap between the breaths.

Pay attention to these gaps.

Be present in the gap,

And present as the gap.

In this way, you will discover the true nature of silence;

You will know infinity;

You will become the source of all life.

....

The mystery is first mentioned in the *Vigyan Bhairava Tantra*, an ancient text from India, in which Shiva gives to his consort Parvati 108 portals to the infinite. This is the first of the portals he delivers.

Our life begins with the first breath, and we return to infinity with the last. Between these two, we incarnate as sentient beings.

The breath comes in and goes out almost a billion times in an average lifetime. The breath is a movement of energy; it is our relationship to the environment. The in-breath is a nourishing, a taking in, an absorbing; it charges the body. We receive; we are reborn. In that receiving, we are in relationship to the outer world; we are in twoness: a me and a not-me.

On the out-breath, there is expulsion; there is expression. Speech always occurs on the out-breath. Again, we are in relationship to what is outside us, but now we are giving to the world, we are letting go. With each out-breath there is a small death. Once again, in that relationship there is a separation, a me and a not-me.

We receive, we give, we absorb, we expel, and in each of these waves we are created again.

In the tiny gap between these two lies a portal to the mysterious dimension where you cease to exist as a fixed entity. Neither giving nor receiving, there is no more relationship, no more outer and inner, no more me and no more not-me. You have become Oneness.

Try this practice each day for a few minutes at a time. It is the key to true meditation.

5

Remember Spaciousness

LEVEL OF DIFFICULTY ***

At any time of the day,
When going about your daily routine,
Stop what you are doing.
If you need to, close your eyes.
Remember a time when you felt most spacious,
Most silent, most expansive.
Consciously remember the feeling in the body;
Notice the way the breath is, just now.
Remember the place where you were,
The people you were with, the sounds, the smells.
With all of you, return to the memory of infinite space.
Now let go of the circumstances of the memory,
And be that space itself.

....

Whether you habitually define yourself as awake or asleep, whether you think of yourself as a spiritual adept or a novice, you have had moments of expansive consciousness. Everyone has. At the peak of lovemaking, perhaps when meeting a great teacher, in meditation, or in sport, we have all had glimpses of reality without the fixation of the mind. Thoughts stop, and the boundaries between the me and the not-me fade and dissolve.

Whenever you allow yourself to remember a moment like this, the brain functioning shifts in order to recapture the memory. The activity of the parietal lobes decreases, and the frontal lobes become more dominant, particularly on the left side. Some research suggests that these changes are immediate when we access a memory of this kind. In order to experience anything, or remember anything, there has to be a change in the brain. Researchers like Dr. Andrew Newberg at the University of Pennsylvania and Dr. Richard Davidson at the University of Wisconsin have started to establish links between certain patterns in brain functioning and the subjective state that Newberg labels as "absolute unitary being."

You can explore this practice alone, by remembering an opening into spaciousness, or you can practice with a friend, by describing such a memory aloud.

After a few minutes of recollection, stop and notice how you are experiencing this moment.

6

Enter the Darkness

LEVEL OF DIFFICULTY ****

Create a room that is perfectly dark.
You might need to tape black plastic over the windows,
And lay a towel at the bottom of the door.
Make it so dark that you can sit with your eyes open
And see not a single chink of light.
Now sit in that darkness, with your eyes open,
And drink in the blackness.
Make friends with darkness,
Reach out into it, and let it soak into you.
Stare with open eyes into the blackness.
Start with an hour.
You can build up to sitting in darkness for many hours,
or even days.

....

It is said that this meditation was taught by the Essenes, who some say were the teachers of Jesus. The great Russian mystic Georges Gurdjieff also used this with his students, and it is also found in Tibetan Buddhism. Darkness is the abode of mystery; it is from where we arise, and it is where we return every night. Every child starts his or her life in the womb, in nine months of darkness. Every seed germinates in the darkness of the soil. Every new dawn, every new meeting with the busyness of the world emerges out of the darkness of the night.

Most meditation places much more emphasis on light: we associate it with the upper chakras, and see it as our goal. Most people fear the dark. Hence, we have created an artificially illuminated world: in a city like New York or Los Angeles, it is never dark; it just shifts from natural light to artificial light.

When you become friendly and comfortable with darkness, something very deep in you can relax, and fear dissolves. Darkness initiates you into the world of the night, into the world of dreams and the unknown. In the beginning, all kinds of fears and freaky images will visit you. You may see snakes or monsters, or remember the most terrifying scenes from murder movies. But this will pass. It only comes because we have pushed darkness away so completely. Then another phase will come, where you will feel the darkness to be your mother, to be safe and nurturing and all around you.

I lived for more than a year in Bali. They have no psychiatrists or psychologists in their culture, and a much lower incidence of mental illness than the rest of the world. If someone begins to show signs of mental imbalance, they are lovingly taken to a dark room for two or three days, and when they emerge they are completely healed. Darkness has a tremendous power to nourish us, to settle us, to rejuvenate us. When you can allow outer darkness to enter you, it has the power to heal almost anything.

Try this for a few days or weeks, and see how your life changes.

Section Two
Insight Practices

REAL INSIGHT IS IMMEDIATELY LIBERATING. There is no time delay between insight and freedom.

But we need to recognize the difference between insight and understanding. Simply changing our understanding adds another layer to an existing web of concepts. Understanding often explains why we experience suffering or separation, but leaves it in place, just as it was. "My moon is in Gemini, and my Venus is squaring Jupiter" may make my life more explicable, but it offers little or no freedom from the constraint of limitation.

We seek understanding in order to do things differently. It is a process in the mind. Things don't work out, so we stop and think about them; we strategize. Eventually we realize our mistake and learn how to go about it in another way. Understanding is the basis for changes in action. It is necessary if one wants to learn to make more money, to improve health, and to make things in the physical world work more efficiently.

But insight is not like that. Insight does not happen in the mind at all. It is the product of pure seeing. Instead of an "uh-huh" moment, it is an "aha!" moment. Insight does not solve problems, it dissolves them. True insight requires no further action; it is an end in itself. It shifts us from the fictions created in the mind to reality itself.

The practices in this section will invite you to ask questions that we usually avoid. They will push you not toward changing things, but toward seeing them as they are and ceasing to struggle with that which does not exist.

7

Who Am I?

LEVEL OF DIFFICULTY ***

Be still and listen to the sounds around you.
The sounds are heard, aren't they? Heard perfectly.
Now shift the attention from the sound to that which is hearing the sounds.
What is that?
What sound does that itself make?
Ask yourself, who am I?

Now feel the sensations in the body, just as they are:
The breathing, the places of tightness and relaxation, pleasure and pain.
Let the attention shift, from the sensation in the body
To that which is feeling the body.
What is that which feels?
What is that which says "my body"?
And ask, who am I?

Let the eyes be gently open.
Look, see what is here.
Notice the shape of it, the color of it, the form of it.
Now let the attention shift from the object to that which sees.
What is that which sees?
Again, ask yourself, who am I?

Whatever arises to be experienced,

Shift your attention from the object to the experiencer.

Seek out your own presence, and discover what that is.

....

All our life we use the terms "I" and "mine" and "me." We talk about my body, my thoughts, my mind, my family, my money, my life. We know what the body is, we know what a thought is, but do we know *who* claims to own these things? As long as this question remains unexamined, we remain trapped in a world of limitation, fully identified with things that have a beginning and an end in time.

When you start to inquire in this way, you may pass through many layers, rather like peeling an onion. Every time you ask the question, "Who am I?" the mind will kick up an answer. "I am a man or a woman, I am rich or poor, I am educated or a simple person." But do not stop with any of these answers. Keep asking and going deeper. To this question, all the answers given by the mind are false. You may shift from identifying with the body to identifying with your thoughts, believing that you are the thinking mind. But that, too, is being experienced. You may drop deeper, into an identification with feelings. But feelings also are passing, coming and going. Finally, you come to the label "me." Who am I? Me. I am me.

Stay with this "me." Try to find it; try to investigate its real nature. You may be surprised to find that it is a challenge to locate a "me." It cannot be found. It simply is not there. And yet this moment *is* being experienced; sounds *are* being heard; form and movement *are* being seen. In the absence of any entity to be found, what remains?

This simple practice returns you home to yourself, to infinity.

8

Is It True?

DIFFICULTY **

When you notice yourself needing to be right,
When you notice your mind is strongly attached to any
conclusion,
Stop and ask yourself, "Is it true?"
Do I really know this?
Is this an absolute, objective, unchanging fact?
Would every sane person in the world agree that it is so?
Or is it simply opinion?
When the mind says, "There's not enough time,"
Ask, "Is it true?"
Do I really know that?
Can that be nailed down as a fact?
Would everyone agree?
When your mind says, "No one likes me,"
Again ask, "Is it true?"
Would everyone agree?
Does everyone feel that way?

When that which had been taken as fact is seen as merely
opinion,
And when that opinion is seen as an optional extra to this very
moment,
Discover what remains true beyond dispute.

. . . .

We carry so many unexamined assumptions in the mind. The challenge for "educated" and "cultured" humanity is that we easily confuse conclusions arrived at through thinking with reality itself. To examine and question the mind is freedom *from* the mind, and freedom from the mind, even for a moment, is to discover reality as it is. Pay attention to everything your mind puts forth as fact. Question everything you believe.

Once you recognize that the mind's assumptions are not absolutely true, please be aware that this does not mean that the opposite is therefore true. When the mind says that there is not enough money, you can ask, "Is it true?" and realize that this was only a belief. This does not necessarily mean that there definitely *is* enough money—that would also be a conclusion of the mind. Neither assumption can be taken as absolute. Questioning belief allows us to drop out of mental conclusions altogether, and to experience things just as they are. This is the way that small babies know life, and how great sages know life, and it is the way that we also can know life—if we are willing to question the mind.

You can do this practice alone or with a friend. If you do it alone, use the practice for a specific period of time, perhaps five minutes, and then relax for a while. If you keep it up for too long, you may start to feel a strain. You can also make an agreement with your partner or a close friend: any time that either of you hears the other state an opinion as if it is absolute fact, you can ask this question: "Is it true?" In this way, you support each other in freedom from the mind, and the relationship itself becomes a means of liberation.

9

Could You Let It Go?

LEVEL OF DIFFICULTY **

> When caught up in a strong belief,
> Needing to be liked, to be right about something,
> Or stuck in a strong emotion, ask yourself,
> "Could I, just could I, let it go?"
> Could you abandon your position?
> Could you open your clenched fist
> And allow whatever is held there to drop to the floor?
> Are you willing for your position to be defeated,
> Even when you think that you are right?
> When you have no position left,
> Knowing nothing,
> How does the world smell to you now?

....

During the Second World War, there was a street in London where certain families had not spoken to each other for decades. They had clung obsessively to resentments of transgressions long past, from one generation to the next. As London was mercilessly bombarded during the blitz, these families were forced to share the same air raid shelter. Faced with the same mortal threat, it took no time at all for them to forget their grievances. Friendships were struck up. People who had not spoken for years began to support each other, help each other, swap jokes, and laugh together.

So much of what we think hinders us is actually optional, necessary only in the mind. If your life depended on it, you could let it go.

This practice is not intended to put you under pressure to let things go. That only creates resistance. The exercise is simply to inquire and evaluate, in a relaxed way, if it is possible to let it go. This discrimination, between what is obligatory and what is optional, is liberation.

Letting go does not happen primarily in the mind—it happens in the body. You do not need to decide to let go; you need only ask yourself if it is possible. In the recognition of this possibility, something happens in the body: a deep sigh, a muscle spasm, or a release of tension you might not have even known was there, and what had seemed to be a prison becomes a choice again. There is no need to know where a belief comes from, or to try to change it in any way, or to understand anything at all. It is enough to feel into the essence of any contraction. That alone will release tremendous energy. That very energy becomes awakening and connects us to what is real.

10

Would I Still Exist?

LEVEL OF DIFFICULTY ***

Take some time to reflect:

Who have you defined yourself to be?

You can write your answers on paper,

Or practice with a friend, and ask your friend to make
notes for you.

I'm a plumber. I'm intelligent. I'm wealthy. I'm uneducated.
I'm a liberal.

Now go back down the list, and for each of these statements,

Ask yourself, "If I stopped defining myself in this way, would I
still exist?"

Or ask your friend to go back down the list with you.

"If I were no longer a plumber, would I still exist?"

"If I no longer thought of myself as a father, would I still be here?"

"If I no longer defined myself as intelligent, would I still exist?"

Take your time to work through all the labels you have placed
upon yourself,

And find out if any of them can really define you or
contain you.

When all labels have been cast aside, discover what remains.

....

This practice will transform your relationship to your identity. For
some of your answers, you'll get an immediate clear "yes." For example, "If I were no longer a plumber, would I still exist?" Yes,

you could always go into selling life insurance. Some may be a little stickier: "If I were no longer a father, would I still exist?" You might have to carefully remember your days before you had children, and ask yourself if the core of who you are now and the core of who you were then is the still same. You might have to imagine what it would be like if one day you woke up and found that your entire experience of parenting was just a dream. Disorienting as it might be, would you still be here?

Some answers will be even more difficult: "I am a man." It might take you several minutes of feeling deeper even than your gender identity to decide if you'd still exist without the gender you are used to. Some of your answers may be conceptual, like "I am light," or "I am consciousness." When you ask, "Would I still exist?" you may feel that this answer points to something deeper than the other labels. You can change the question to "Would I still exist without this thought, without this concept?"

Whether you do this exercise alone or with a friend, you will need some time for it to go deep. If it does, stop and feel your own presence when you have let go of all definitions. Are you still here? Can you still feel and see and hear? Take some time to relax into knowing the face you had before you were born.

We perform myriad roles during our lifetime. Each one may be necessary, even creative or enjoyable, but each can also become a prison if we become completely identified with the role and forget our deeper nature.

11

Write Yourself a Letter

LEVEL OF DIFFICULTY **

Next time you feel clear, centered, and silent,
Perhaps after a deep meditation, or when you are
deeply rested,
When things reveal themselves to you just as they are
In their natural perfection, not needing any improvement,
Write yourself a letter.
This is a letter you will read when you next feel confused,
When you are anxious, when you are caught up in resisting
things as they are.
Follow your heart as to what to write.
It might be insights;
It might be statements of appreciation; it might even be jokes.
Put the letter in a safe place: in the drawer next to your bed,
In the back of a favorite book, or wherever you keep sacred things.

When you feel that your world is falling apart,
That you meet obstacles everywhere,
That you lack the strength to carry on,
Go find the letter.
You might even have several,
In different places in your house.
Read, receive, digest.
Take counsel from a true friend

Who loves you in this moment
More than you love yourself.

....

When you feel lost or confused, it is natural to look for wisdom and advice from outside yourself. We turn to our friends, our counselors, our teachers, to point the way. Many times, this is a great thing to do: we can be teachers and guides to each other all the time. But do your advisors ever all agree? Do they know you well enough and everything you have passed through, to really know all of who you are, to really give you sound advice? Ultimately, the most reliable source of wisdom is within your own heart.

When you write this letter, be extremely loving and compassionate with yourself. It is not a moral lecture or chastisement; write it with compassion. Write to yourself as someone you love, respect, forgive, and wish the best for.

When you read the letter at a later time, read it slowly and carefully, digesting every word. Feel it as a gift from a friend who loves you more than you could ever know, and, in that moment, more than you love yourself. This conversation with the divine, with the space and stillness of your true nature, is between you as a wave and you as the ocean, not between you and another wave.

Write these letters often. They will deepen your compassion and forgiveness.

12

Write Your Own Obituary

LEVEL OF DIFFICULTY ***

One day you will die, and you will be remembered.

What will you be remembered for?

Take a few minutes to write your own obituary

As you would like it to appear one day.

He was a loving, caring father and a good husband.

He lived with courage and never abandoned his deepest integrity.

She gave everything to her community,

And her actions touched many lives.

How do you want to be remembered?

Write your obituary: one or two paragraphs.

When you're finished, read it through.

Is the way that you're living your life today creating the life this

obituary describes?

Is the way that you live now consistent with the way you want

to be remembered?

Take a few small steps today to bring your life in tune

with your vision.

....

My teacher, H. W. L. Poonjaji, once said that there is only one thing that gets in the way of living in alignment with the heart. Many people were gathered together that day, and he asked them what they thought it was. What is it that most holds us back from living in the integrity of the heart? "The mind," someone said. "The ego," said another. "Greed," said another. Everybody in the room had some idea of what was in the way. None of them said what he had in mind. When it became quiet, he said, "There is only one thing that is in the way of living in the integrity of the heart: distraction."

When you start a new job, or discover you are going to have a child, or move into a new house, or fall in love, you often have a strong sense of vision, of purpose, of how things could be. But we all suffer from distraction. We lose sight of our integral vision in the face of life's momentary desires and pleasures, the hundred thousand small details that constantly come and go.

There have been a few people who have died, for a few minutes only, and who have then been brought back to life. Their hearts stopped beating; they were physically dead. The most remarkable thing that survivors of such "near death experiences" have in common is that they are cured of distraction. They remember, in a much deeper sense than just thinking about it, why they are alive, what they came for, and what really makes a difference in life.

Give yourself the gift of a near death experience today. Die while alive, as the Zen poet Bunan suggested, and be absolutely dead.

Use this simple exercise to bring the way that you live now into alignment with a life lived without regret.

Section Three

Daily-Routine Practices

IT IS NORMAL TO WANT to segregate what we think of as *spirituality* and what we think of as *normal life*. Meditation is something you do on a cushion. Yoga is something you do on a mat. The rest of life is activity you do on caffeine and adrenaline. We create boundaries in this way. For example, going to church, spending time in nature, or being in an intimate relationship are designated as contexts where we can feel the divine; what we can experience while standing in line at the bank, doing the laundry, or driving to work is another matter.

The practices in this section invite you to break down that distinction and feel your deeper connection in the most unlikely of contexts. Our daily routine is usually focused around getting things done: we make lists and check tasks off one by one. But as soon as we eliminate one or two things, we add several more. In this way, we live in an eternal state of striving for a future of completion, rather like trying to climb a mountain of loose rubble, where with every step up we also slip backward. We thus do many things carelessly or on automatic pilot, because we are only doing them to get them done and move on to the next thing.

The best way to leap before you look is to reverse this habit and bring your attention to what is happening now, rather than the fruits of your actions later. When we bring a spirit of practice to the daily routine, we start to do things more carefully. Now we are not just standing in line at the bank to get some cash to buy some gas to drive to the store to buy some food to make dinner to be able to relax and rest. We are standing in line to show up fully, to be available to this moment ultimately to be available to all of life.

The seven practices in this section will help you bring an element of freshness to the tired habits of your day-to-day life.

13

Slow Down

LEVEL OF DIFFICULTY *

In the midst of any activity during the day,
Raising a cup of tea to your lips,
Reaching out to answer the phone,
Continue doing exactly as you have been doing,
But slow your movements down.
Move at a quarter of the usual speed, or even less.
Become aware of the minute details involved:
The movements of individual muscles,
The thoughts and feelings that accompany each action.
Practice in this way for several minutes.
Then continue with your day.

....

When each activity becomes only a step in a process, so we can cross it off the mental list and move on to the next thing, then everything becomes automated, happening as quickly as possible. We just want to get it out of the way. Certainly, it is like that for most people when dialing a phone number, brushing their teeth, checking their e-mail, or operating a computer or another machine. In a restaurant, cooking and serving food often gets to be like that for the people working there, as they wind up doing the same thing over and over again.

For some of us, even meeting new people can become automated and fast: such as for the person behind the cash register in the supermarket, or a politician shaking hundreds of hands, or an author signing books at an event. We can even get sped up and automatic in our parenting, in art or creativity, and, scary as it may seem, even in our lovemaking.

The simplest way to restore conscious presence to any activity is to slow it down to a quarter of the usual speed. While taking a shower, reach out for the shampoo or the soap slowly enough that you really feel the water cascading on your body and smell the perfume of the shampoo. You will notice how much there is to experience, just in your small shower stall. Drinking a cup of tea, or eating an apple, if you slow it all down, will reveal an entire world of sensory delight locked away in these small acts. When talking to a friend, if you consciously take a longer time to say the same thing, pausing between each small phrase, you will immediately discover the tidal waves of feeling and energy flowing between the two of you, in just the simplest of exchanges.

If you choose to practice in this way, try slowing down many times a day for a week to ten days. It will restore awe to your world.

14

Standing in Line

LEVEL OF DIFFICULTY **

Waiting in line at the bank,
At a fast food restaurant,
Or at the gate at the airport,
Sink yourself completely into this moment.
Feel your feet planted on the ground.
Place your heels about shoulder width apart,
Turn your feet slightly inward
With your weight balanced equally on each foot,
Knees relaxed, not locked.
Open your chest.
Breathe and listen to all the sounds around you.
Take everything in.
Feel the whole environment through your skin.
Become sensitive to the atmosphere of the place.
Breathe a little deeper and notice the smells.
Expand your vision so that you become aware of everything
around you.
Relax.
Finally, feel even deeper than all of this,
Into your own presence,
Into that which is hearing and feeling and seeing.
Let that presence expand and permeate everything around you.
Expand and become the living blessing.

....

There are so many times in the day that we think of as "down time." You're not doing anything, but waiting for the next thing to happen. It is habitual to fidget our way through such moments: to shut out the environment and become distracted in thought, on the cell phone, or just spacing out. Unless we have something specific to focus on, it is often our habit to unfocus and follow random thoughts in all directions. We value any random speaking, thinking, or action over presence in the moment.

With this practice, you can punctuate your activity with short blasts of meditative presence. In the beginning, you may feel uncomfortable, not unlike when you are trying to quit smoking or any other kind of addictive behavior. It can feel almost unbearable to be present in the body; you may feel like you want to burst or scream. But the longer and more often you can do this practice, the easier it becomes, until meditative pauses become something to look forward to, and they even happen on their own.

Moments like this, standing in line or waiting to board a plane, are, in fact, great opportunities to be unconditionally present with what is, to practice opening yourself without reservation to reality exactly as it is in this moment. The gift of presence can be practiced. It needs to be valued as a gift and nurtured. Whenever you find yourself waiting, remember that it is an opportunity for benevolence. Your entire body will respond immediately to this invitation, relaxing, aligning, and revitalizing itself.

15

Get It All Done Before Nine

LEVEL OF DIFFICULTY ***

Every now and then,
Set your alarm for very, very early in the morning,
Long before everyone else gets up.
Four thirty or five o'clock will be fine.
The night before, make a list of tasks that you've gotten behind on,
Paying bills, responding to e-mail, whatever.
Make a list that is all doable in a few hours.
When you awaken, stretch your body, take a shower, and have a cup of tea.
Put yourself into a focus mode,
And work through the tasks, checking them off one by one.
Aim for a sense of completion by nine o'clock, and then stop.
Take a walk
Or sit quietly and be with yourself.
Now notice the space inside yourself.

....

Getting caught up on things, particularly early in the morning, is not just an act in the interest of efficiency; it causes the pituitary gland and the hypothalamus to release endorphins into the brain, a kind of natural opiate that creates a sense of well-being and ease.

When we have a long list of things to do, when we feel under pressure, we live in a psychological future. "As soon as I have done this and this and this, then I can relax." Living in a sense of incompletion creates psychological pressure: it releases stress hormones like adrenaline and cortisone into the body, which cause us to feel constant imminent danger. Not only does this sense of having a lot to do create psychological tension and stress in the body, but the very feeling of pressure causes us to accumulate more things to do. Crisis creation is addictive.

As far as we know, other animals do not live in this way. A dolphin or an eagle lives in a psychological present, where there is one thing to do or nothing to do. Hence, wild animals do not suffer from stress, or if they do for a brief period (as when being chased by a predator), they know how to release it very quickly. Only domestic animals, once they are trained for specific tasks and have goals to accomplish in psychological time, show signs of stress like humans beings do.

Of course, one time-tested way to move out of psychological time is to take a vacation or go on a retreat. The important thing is to always leave behind your cell phone and laptop, and within one or two days you will forget your to-do list. This practice is another way to shift out of psychological time. If you rise very early and get your tasks done before the rest of the world is stirring, a shift that allows deep rest will happen in your brain. In the clarity of the hours before the world stirs, you will surprise yourself with how easy things become.

16

Adopt a New Personality in the Supermarket

LEVEL OF DIFFICULTY *****

With a friend, go to a supermarket,

But not your local supermarket, where you may know people.

Drive a little way to the nearest town.

Take the shopping cart and enter the supermarket.

Your friend will be observing you,

And will give you a mood, a personality trait, or a

quality to embody.

It could be *paranoid, lustful, excited, antagonizing, interested,*

or *ecstatic.*

It can be anything your friend can think of.

Take five minutes to put your whole body into this quality.

What kind of thoughts do you have? How do you move? How

do you look at people?

Everything becomes involved in the quality that your friend has

given you.

If the word is "paranoid," look at the frozen peas with suspicion.

Use your body to fully feel fear.

Look at the other shoppers with certainty of their

bad intentions.

Do not interact with other people or disturb them, just feel this

quality in yourself.

After five minutes, stop, breathe, and shake your body, loosen up.

Then take another word and another five minutes.

After you've changed personalities five or six times,

Discover what it is like to walk through the supermarket
wearing no personality at all.
Then you can exchange roles and be a witness for your friend.

....

The purpose of this practice is to create some space and playfulness around what you consider to be your personality. We get used to certain moods and personality traits, like an old pair of sneakers that we hold on to long after they've outworn their usefulness. Sometimes it is easier to see that in other people than in yourself. When you meet someone who is habitually grumpy or speedy or critical, it may be obvious to you that it is just a habit, which could easily be broken. We get so attached to these habits that we start to think that this is who we are, that nothing else is possible. This is clearly not true. Anyone who has acted on a stage knows that it is not so, that it is possible to try something else. Whenever you consciously take on a personality that is different from your habitual one, you are able to loosen the whole grip of the personality and discover that you are actually much less defined than you thought you were. Many people speak of being on stage as one of the greatest spiritual disciplines, because they are consciously taking on a role and letting it go again. This allows you to discover who you are beyond all such roles.

This simple practice can be fun, especially when you do it with a friend. It makes something that is happening unconsciously anyway into a conscious practice. You can consciously take moods on and off, like changing a T-shirt, instead of letting them run your life. You discover that there is much more freedom than you imagined.

And, most important, you discover the possibility of taking the T-shirt off and not replacing it with anything: the capability to stand naked in front of reality as it is. You might also notice that the same supermarket looks different through the eyes of different moods, that people will approach and look at you differently.

In this freedom, you discover that the way you experience the world is a projection of your own mind.

17

Mess with Your Sleep

LEVEL OF DIFFICULTY ****

Discover the innate assumptions you have about your
sleeping patterns,
Then change them for a short period.
Are you "not a morning person"?
Do you "need a good eight hours"?
Do you "turn into a pumpkin after nine in the evening"?
Do you know for sure that these things are true?
Perhaps with the help of your partner, discover what your
habits are,
And then, for a few days, change them.
Experiment with new habits.
If you have been going to bed late, try to go to bed early.
If you have been sleeping in, get up before dawn.
If you have been getting by on a few hours sleep, pamper
yourself and sleep more.
If you have been sleeping long, sleep less.
As you change your sleeping patterns,
Notice what happens to your relationship to reality.

....

Rhythms of sleep and waking have enormous influence on the way
we experience things, and they tend to be addictive. In India, the
most ancient science of medicine known to humankind is called
Ayurveda. Ayurveda recognizes three kinds of disposition or *dosha:*

vata, pitta, and *kapha.* Vata people tend to be volatile, speedy, and nervous. They have a predisposition toward insomnia, but the vata condition is also aggravated by not sleeping. Kapha is characterized by docility. Kapha people have a preference for sleeping a lot, but the more they sleep, the more out of balance they become. It can be helpful to know which kind of person you are, to discover your dominant doshic balance, or *prakriti.* If you recognize yourself to have a vata disposition, for example, use rest as a spiritual practice, particularly by going to bed early. If you recognize yourself to be predisposed toward kapha, discipline yourself to wake up early. Pitta people are fiery and forceful, often driven; practice taking frequent naps during the day. By addressing imbalance and addiction in the cycles of rest and inactivity, you will come deeper into wholeness.

Be gentle with this practice, and use it only for short periods to recreate balance. It is important to respect the needs of the body. This is a practice that would be good to do with the support of your partner or a close friend, or a support group (see practice 68). The purpose of this practice is to temporarily shift habits in the body, not to try to permanently change your constitution.

18

Take the Day Off

LEVEL OF DIFFICULTY ***

Every one or two months,
Take a day where you do absolutely nothing,
Just as you would do if you had the flu,
But do it when you're not sick.
Switch off the phones; shut down the computer.
If necessary, stay in bed all day.
Do as little as possible.
Just lie still and give the body and the psyche a chance for
deep healing.
If you're married, if you live with your family or friends,
You could even alternate stillness days:
One of you could completely take care of the other, including
meals in bed, then switch.
If possible, refrain from watching television or other
distractions.
Just lie still and give all of yourself,
Including your senses,
Twenty-four hours of undiluted rest.

....

Most people get sick every now and then. You get a fever, maybe
a sore throat and a headache, and life forces you to go to bed and
lie down until you feel better. As we become more attuned to our
bodies, we realize that often things only get that bad because we've

been pushing ourselves too hard. Some conscious businesses allow their employees wellness days instead of sickness days, days that can be used to restore the body to health, whether you are sick or not. Try to give yourself a stillness day every few weeks. Be totally immersed in rest. You may find yourself needing far fewer days off for being sick.

During this practice, you may experience feelings of restlessness, or even guilt about doing nothing. You may be overcome with compulsive needs to take care of things, like cleaning out the closet or doing all the laundry. When these seemingly urgent projects arise, bring your attention back to the body itself, to the sensations from which these impulses arise, and feel them completely. You may notice burning or vibrating in different parts of your body as you release stress. Feel all of this, and it will pass. It is the body's way of letting go. Sooner or later you will fall into a deeper place, and you will want to sleep and do nothing. It does not take very long for the body to come back to its natural state.

19

Discard the Old

LEVEL OF DIFFICULTY **

Take some time to discard what is no longer needed.
You could start with your clothes.
Be honest: if you have not worn it in over a year,
Put it in a bag for the thrift store.
Look through your books: how many will you ever read again?
Go through your music, your movies, your knickknacks.
If something is just taking up storage space, get it out
of your life.
Take the things you can let go of to the garbage or the
thrift store.
Then, sit quietly for a few minutes and
Feel the space you have created in your life.
Feel the space that has also been opened
Inside yourself.
Do this practice often,
Until all clutter is gone,
And you can enjoy simplicity.

....

In many ways, your immediate environment is a reflection of, as well as a cause of, how you feel inside. Spring cleaning is a powerful way to provoke natural emptiness and presence. When you discard old photographs, papers, books, or clothes, it allows you to also let go of structures in the mind and psyche associated with those things. Experiment for yourself, and see how differently this simple practice can allow you to feel in yourself.

You may experience some resistance to this practice, tinges of regret as you are on the way to the garbage can. We are born into the world empty-handed, and one day we will also leave that way. As a newborn baby, you have no identity. You have no style of dress, no preferred make of car, no favorite musicians or movies. As you collect these things over a lifetime, so do you become seemingly more and more solid, defined and different from other people. In fact, that is all that makes you absolutely unique, a different set of likes and dislikes from other people.

Whenever you let go of something from the past, you pass through a small death. It hurts a little. When you throw away old sneakers you once loved, or a vinyl record you listened to in college, it can feel like a part of you is dying. And it is true, it is a small death of identity. But these small deaths can also be enjoyed; they are a death of the temporal identity, of that which must sooner or later die, but they are also the rebirth in you of something eternal, of that which can never die.

Remember, whenever you let go of the old, sit with yourself for a while afterward and enjoy the space. Enjoy the taste of freedom.

Section Four

Body Practices

THE BODY IS ABSOLUTELY INNOCENT, like an animal or a small baby. Your body cannot lie. That's why kinesiology, or muscle testing, usually works as a way to access a truth deeper than thinking. It is why lie detector tests portray a deeper truth than what the mind would have us believe—or try to make others believe. The voice of the body is totally trustworthy.

The body lives anchored to the present moment. Never for one second of its life has it strayed into past or future. It knows nothing of these things: it is always right here. Only thoughts run into past and future. In fact, the mind lives *only* in time. It has no connection at all to the present. So, when we connect to the body, we are connecting to the now. The body is part of the earth. It has been created by eating the harvest of the earth, and every day it excretes what it no longer needs back into the earth. When the body dies, it will decompose and become earth again. Thus, the body is also our connection to the earth, our grounding rod to reality as it is. The body is not in relationship to the earth, it is part of the earth.

Generally, we take the body for granted. We easily neglect its needs, ignore the messages it gives us. We are often harsh with the body, pushing it beyond its limits, letting it go longer than it would like without proper rest or nourishment or water. Just like a horse, the body is patient and loyal, and it tries to do everything that we ask of it, even when we ask more than it can give.

The body is a miracle. That it breathes on its own, that it pumps blood inside itself, that it digests food by itself, are all miracles. The body is matter energized by a mystery that defies our understanding: the miracle of life.

By bringing awareness to the body in the ways described here, you can restore the body to its natural capacity, to be a temple for presence, a container for infinity. Do these practices lovingly and gently. The body is a friend, absolutely innocent and honest.

20

Feel Tension and Welcome It

LEVEL OF DIFFICULTY **

Scan your body with awareness.
Seek out a place of tension or discomfort,
And rest there with your attention.
Feel this place exactly as it is.
Feel it, be with it, just as it is.
Feel it not so that it will go away,
But with an invitation that it may stay forever.
Kiss the tension with the softness of awareness.
Bring the breath all the way into this place,
As though you are pouring water into a dry sponge.
Wait, linger, until the flower opens,
Until your awareness is completely there.
Move on to another place of tension,
And then another.
Discover the lotus growing in the mud.

....

We generally have an unfriendly relationship to sensations in the body. Tension and pain are the body's cries for attention, just like the call of a newborn baby who knows no words. When we try to ignore the body's signals, whether directly with painkillers or just blocking them out through distraction, we cut off our connection to the real, to the world that can be truly known only through the senses. This tendency to block out the sensations in the body goes so deep that we rarely even know what it means to experience the body as it is. A fleeting feeling arises, and it is met with an immediate thought that it should not be this way. *This sensation is bad; this one is good.* One single thought can set in motion a pattern of tension, for instance in the pelvis, solar plexus, or chest, that shuts down the flow of blood and energy in such a way as to almost completely inhibit our capacity to feel. Only numbness and thoughts are left. When this knee-jerk reaction occurs, stop for a moment. Retrace your steps. Whether you're sitting in your office, waiting in traffic, or lying in bed, return to that which has been locked out. Open the door with welcome, and consciously linger with that which has been banished. If we acknowledge and welcome tension and pain, not in an effort to make them go away but with a loving embrace, they will transform themselves. It is in this embrace of our greatest discomfort that we are initiated into the body of bliss, into wisdom of the body.

You cannot try to relax: it is only counterproductive. The more you try to make any part of your body relax, the more tense it will become. The body relaxes through just the opposite: through feeling tension and welcoming it completely. It is a paradox: the more you are all right with being tense, the more relaxed you will become, and the more you try to relax, the more tense you will become.

Relaxation is the natural state of the body. It is where it returns to when it is left alone. A relaxed body is the natural temple for relaxed and natural consciousness: free, limitless, and experiencing spontaneous Oneness with all that it encounters.

21

Push the Body to Its Limits

LEVEL OF DIFFICULTY ****

The next time you are running,
Run as fast as you can without stopping
Until you have exhausted your limits.
If you are doing push-ups,
Or any kind of weight training,
Keep going until you cannot do another repetition.
When holding a certain posture, like a yoga pose
Or a position in chi kung,
Hold it until the body cannot hold it any longer.
When you are dancing, dance until you cannot
dance any longer.
When you have reached your limits,
Stop, lie down, and relax completely.
Open your arms wide and feel the open sky in your chest.
Be ready to be surprised by what is here, beyond your limits.

....

Small children and animals live like this. They expend energy with
totality, and then they stop completely. It is because there is no
mind interfering. The mind will tell you that you have reached
your limits long before the body will agree, and will try to set limitations for you. Long-distance runners know this very well: they
call it the *second wind*. If you continue beyond the limits imposed
by the mind, you will access a new level of energy that you did not

know was there. You will discover new resources of energy, and, if you explore them, they will lead you beyond the mind and into the natural state.

Most of us push our bodies to their limits, but in a prolonged way: we do not stop to give our bodies a break for hours or sometimes even days. This is another way that the mind imposes itself on the natural world of the body: by working without taking a break for many hours. The mind enters into a push/pull relationship with the body, rather like driving with your foot on the accelerator and the brake at the same time. The mind keeps pushing the body forward, never allowing it to rest, but at the same time holding it back from fully expending its energy.

This practice is very different. You do it only for a few minutes at a time, and then you stop completely. As soon as you push your body to its true limits in any way, a gate opens, and you discover the capacity of the body to be a vessel for infinity.

Of course, if you have any kind of physical condition or any doubt about using this practice, you should consult with a qualified medical professional.

22

Yawn

LEVEL OF DIFFICULTY **

At any time of the day,
Evening or night,
Make yawning into a conscious practice.
No need to wait until you feel like it:
Yawn anyway.
Open your jaw wide and stretch it.
Make it a *big* yawn.
Take a deep breath, into the lower part of the belly.
With the exhale, make a sound: "Aaaaah!"
Do it again.
In less than a minute, the body will respond:
You will continue to yawn naturally.
Notice a change in your breathing rhythm,
And a natural release of the diaphragm.
Do this for about five minutes, three or four
time a day.

....

This simple practice will change everything in just a few minutes. The key is to yawn consciously—not to wait until the body yawns on its own—and to yawn totally, generously, with maximum stretch and sound. If you can, take a short nap after using this practice; if your body needs rest in that moment, it will naturally take what it needs after some conscious yawning.

The benefits of conscious yawning are too many to list here. You will discover just how much this supports presence very quickly on your own. So, here is just a short summary.

Yawning brings fresh oxygen into the body cells, including the eyes and the brain. A really good yawn will contract and expand muscles from the top of your head to the tips of your toes, including the muscles in the neck and shoulders (the trapezii) where we accumulate a great deal of day-to-day tension. It releases tension in the eyes (orbicularis oculi), stimulating the production of refreshing tears that moisten strained eyes. Yawning releases tension in the abdominal and solar plexus area, bringing release to the diaphragm, where we hold much of our habitual emotional tension. It should be no surprise, then, that yawning can easily dissipate funky emotional states. Doctors tell us that yawning changes the pH of the blood, making it more alkaline and reducing the toxicity of the whole system. Chinese medicine advocates yawning as a way to help cleanse the liver and balance the energy in the liver meridian.

If you do this practice regularly for a few weeks, several times a day, you may notice not only that the body feels more relaxed and flowing, but also that you become more attuned to your body's rhythms and needs.

23

Pranayama

LEVEL OF DIFFICULTY ***

Sit comfortably, with your spine as upright as possible.
Let your left hand rest on your left knee
With the palm facing upward.
Bring your right hand up to your nose
And rest your index finger on the tip of the nose.
With your thumb, close your right nostril.
Breathe out normally through your left nostril.
Breathe in normally through your left nostril.
Close you left nostril with your middle and ring fingers
And release the right nostril.
Breathe out normally through your right nostril.
Breathe in normally through your right nostril.
Close your right nostril with your thumb
And release the left nostril again.
Breathe out, and breathe in.
Continue alternating in this way for five minutes.

....

Alternate nostril breathing, one kind of *pranayama*, is one of the most beneficial practices to bring the body into a deeper state of natural presence. *Prana* means life force or breath. *Yama* means practice. Pranayama means to practice with the breath, or life force, in order to bring more energy into the body in such a way that can support awakening or expand life force.

Breathing is one of the few autonomic functions of the body to which you can bring conscious practice. You do not have the same freedom with the digestive system, the heartbeat, or body temperature. The breath is seen by many to be the link between the body, thoughts, feelings, and pure consciousness.

We could fill a whole book with why this is such an important and beneficial practice. Just as with other practices in this section, pranayama brings the breath deeper into the lungs, so we can absorb more oxygen and release accumulated stress. It can make your digestion stronger, strengthen the immune system, and calm and steady the mind. Pranayama will make almost any other practice in this book go deeper, as it gives us greater focus and concentration. For the feeling practices, for example, when we breathe more fully and in a steady rhythm we have greater balance and space to experience all of our feelings.

Above all else, we know that irregular or shallow breathing sets up patterns in the brain that we experience subjectively as random thoughts and internal conflict. Pranayama brings balance to the brain, making it easier for us to experience the silence and space under the mind's activity.

24

Explore Hunger

LEVEL OF DIFFICULTY ****

When you start to feel the first pangs of hunger,

Be still and present for a while.

Feel the sensation of hunger

And let it spread through your whole body.

After some time, you will feel it has a sensual quality to it.

It can become as pleasurable as sexual energy.

Feel the emotions that hunger stimulates in you

And drop deeper into pure enjoyment of the sensation of being hungry.

Make friends with the sensation of hunger.

Do not eat only out of habit;

Wait until you have experienced your hunger for a while.

When your hunger reaches its peak,

Then exercise your body before eating:

Run, bike, or lift weights.

After exercising,

Eat a nutritious meal right away.

Relax fully into the pleasure of satiation.

....

One of the diseases of modern civilization is that we have developed very narrow comfort zones. If a natural sensation like hunger sets in, we try to do something about it immediately. We run to the fridge or the convenience store to fill the gap as soon as it even begins to reveal itself. Today, any bodily sensation we identify as negative must be immediately eradicated.

My good friend Christian Opitz, who has a doctorate in biochemistry from the University of Berlin, devotes himself to educating people on how they can return to the natural rhythms of the body. He has learned much from studying the diet and eating cycles of other mammals, as well as those of indigenous people. He has found that in indigenous societies, hunger is allowed to build during much longer periods of activity than we are accustomed to, which are followed by a cycle of full satiation. He explains that most mammals have two cycles of the autonomic nervous system, one associated with the vagus nerve, and the other associated with the sympathicus nerve. The cycle associated with the sympathicus nerve is one of alertness and energy, of getting things done. It is much more easily dominant when we are hungry. So, the load of our work, the things we want to accomplish, should be done with a feeling of slight hunger. Eating turns on the vagus nerve and initiates a cycle of rest and relaxation. The two rhythms are very important. When we eat out of habit, before we are hungry, they do not alternate any more, they commingle. You can no longer be awake when you need to be, and you also cannot fully relax.

Hunger optimizes your brain for alertness. So, for any kind of meditative exploration, for crisp awareness and a sense of presence, exploring hunger is very helpful.

Of course, if you suffer from hyperglycemia or any other condition closely tied to diet, or if you have any doubts or concerns about using this practice, you should first consult with your licensed healthcare professional.

25

Breathe Totally

LEVEL OF DIFFICULTY *

Notice how you are already breathing in this moment.
Is the breath coming more into the upper part of the body?
Is it reaching the diaphragm?
Or is the breath reaching all the way down to the lower belly?
After just watching the way you are breathing for a couple
of minutes,
Begin to bring some intention to your breathing.
With the in-breath,
Let the lower belly soften and expand.
When the lower belly feels full,
Feel the diaphragm expand with the breath.
Finally, let the chest and lungs fill completely with breath.
Hold the in-breath for a few moments,
Only as long as is comfortable,
Then let the air be expelled fully from the lungs:
First from the chest, then the diaphragm, and then the lower belly.
Just when you think you're done,
Give an extra little push,
And you will find there is even more air to be expelled.
Hold on the out-breath for a few moments, before you
inhale again.
Continue to breathe totally in this way for several minutes.

....

Awareness of the breath and breathing consciously is the basis of all yoga practices. It reduces stress and anxiety, brings fresh oxygen to the blood, and restores us to fully feeling what we are experiencing and to being in the present moment. It is so simple, and it can be done anywhere at any time.

The natural wisdom of the body allows it to breathe totally. At night, whenever you are in dreamless sleep, you naturally start to breathe from the belly. You wake up from a good night's sleep feeling refreshed, new-born. The problems of the night before seem far-off; you have new energy and a new outlook. All this is because you were breathing into the belly for many hours, and the whole system has become rejuvenated as a result.

Our breathing closes down because of our nonstop thinking and our unwillingness to feel. Most of us breathe only halfway, into the chest but not all the way down into the lower belly. We feel less emotional pain that way, but we also feel less alive. We move more into the mental world. It is a vicious cycle: our closing down emotionally leads to restricted breathing, which in turn leads to further shutting down, thought, and emotional disconnect.

When you breathe totally in the way described here, you will feel more, and the feelings will also pass more quickly. Your thoughts will become more transparent—they will seem less real to you, less concrete. You will be fooled less often by the mind. This is a great practice to do when you feel nervous; actors and performers practice in this way to calm themselves and to remain focused. Use this practice frequently, and it will start to become a new way of living.

Section Five

Feeling Practices

....

FOR MILLENNIA, WE HAVE BEEN conditioned not to feel too much. We have become accustomed to stuffing anger, grief, excitement, and even joy down into the cells of the body. Then, once we've done so, we are afraid that they will well up again and explode. We suffer, not so much from feelings themselves, but from the resistance and shame associated with them. Almost everyone is terrified to feel without restraint.

For just as long, spiritual life has been dominated by the masculine psyche. This energy, which is present in all of us, is primarily goal-oriented: it thrives on breaking through obstacles with determination and force to reach a goal of temporary expansion and release. Enlightenment, when it refers to a fixed goal to be reached in the future, is a product of the hypermasculine mind. To the masculine energy, feelings, particularly so-called negative feelings, are obstructions to be managed or eliminated—they get in the way of the agenda of achievement.

As a race, we know very little of feminine spirituality. Historically, it has not been allowed to blossom, and is only really beginning to do so now, as we move into the twenty-first century. The feminine in all of us discovers the divine, not as a goal in the future, but in the unconditional embrace of what is in the now. Just as the masculine seeks to control and sublimate feeling, the feminine thrives in embracing feeling completely. The feeling practices in this section are a way for all of us to return to a balance of masculine and feminine energy. We can reclaim a life that is simultaneously evolving and embracing, endlessly expanding towards greater potential even as it is grounded in the unwavering acceptance and embrace of what is in this moment.

26

Welcome All Feeling

LEVEL OF DIFFICULTY **

Whenever you feel provoked,
Irritated, pulled to make a response,
Stop.
Sit back in the saddle.
Scan your body and notice what you are feeling.
Seek out any areas of strong emotional tension;
Feel what is there. If it helps you, label it:
Sadness, anger, desire, whatever it may be.
Stay with the sensations,
Dropping the story—the why and the because.
Do everything you can to experience what is here,
To the maximum possible degree, for no more than
a few minutes.
Then, relax.
Feel your interiority as though for the first time.
If there's more emotional tension calling to be felt in this moment,
Take a few extra minutes to welcome feeling even more totally.
Keep going until the charge is gone.
Feel yourself now; you are not just a loving person,
You are Love itself.

....

We have all been faced with experiences that seem overwhelming:
the anger of a drunk parent; the thrill of a sexual encounter; the

end of a relationship. We have learned to say "yes" to parts of what we feel, and "no" to the rest. Long ago, we built a wall in the middle of our emotional landscape. Do we still need that wall today?

Say you receive a letter with news of a long-lost friend. He died of AIDS, alone and misunderstood. Your mind races with all the things you could have said, should have said, would have said. Faced with such feelings of hopelessness and regret, our natural reaction is to try to forget them, to push them away.

Stop. Disengage all stories, drop in, and further in. Feel to the core of your grief, beyond where you know any longer what you are grieving for. Feel.

Whatever feeling we say "no" to will get buried in our muscles and digestive organs. Anger, which could have been clean and wild and free, and which would have harmed no one if it were fully felt as an energy, gets pushed down into the body and becomes festering bitterness. It will lash out unexpectedly in all kinds of ways. Grief, which could take us deeply into the vulnerability of the open heart, gets compressed into the diaphragm and chest, making us gray and stooped, constricting our energy.

When we have strong feelings, we often feel faced with an impossible choice: to repress or to express. When we express, we risk hurting someone with an outburst of anger, or dragging someone down with our grief or sadness. If we repress, we shut down not only this feeling arising now, but all feeling and aliveness that was possible as well. To feel is the middle way. To fully feel each thing as it arises is freedom.

Each passing feeling is waiting to be met. Say "yes" to everything you feel, while discarding the irrelevance of the drama. In this *yes*, breathe true freedom.

27

Cradle Negative Feelings Like a Baby
LEVEL OF DIFFICULTY ***

> When you notice yourself caught up in a feeling,
> Like resentment, rejection, or despair,
> Cradle that feeling as though it were a small baby.
> It may even help you to take a cushion and physically cradle
> the feeling in your arms.
> Sing to it.
> Soothe it.
> Let that feeling know that it is accepted, loved, and welcomed.
> In fully accepting grief,
> You become acceptance itself,
> Which is none other than your natural state.

....

Have you ever experienced what happens when a child tries to get your attention when you are busy? Perhaps you are on the phone and need to be undisturbed for a few minutes, and your child comes to you wanting a snack or to play with you. Your child simply wants attention. Have you ever discovered what happens if you say "no"? What if you put your hand over the mouthpiece of the phone, and in a terse whisper tell your child, "Not now, can't you see I'm busy? Don't disturb me now!" Before too long, your child will find a louder and even more disturbing way to get your attention. You can raise your voice, you can get stern and angry, but if you push that child away, sooner or later your child will break something, hurt him or herself, or take it out on someone else. On the other hand, if your child comes to you wanting attention and you give your full attention, take him or her on your knee and give a cuddle, your child will soon feel happy and run and play.

Your feelings are your disowned children. If you take them close, if you cradle them like a baby, they will soon stop disturbing you. They will stop crying for your attention. Grief, when fully embraced, reveals our full depth. Despair, when fully welcomed, becomes unconditional acceptance. Every feeling that has been banished will reveal its inner beauty when it is made to feel welcome and cared for.

Some of these feelings may have been labeled as "negative," which means that they seem like a "no" to life. The place to start is to offer an unconditional "yes" to the perceived "no." In that opening, you become the yes itself. Sooner or later you will come to discover the greatest secret for yourself: there is no such thing as negative energy. Whatever is embraced becomes beautiful, whatever is denied becomes ugly.

28

Express Feeling Free of a Story

LEVEL OF DIFFICULTY ****

For this practice,
You will need to make a compilation
Of many different kinds of music.
Make a playlist on your iPod or computer.
Find some music that is soft and soothing,
Some which is angry and defiant.
Find some that has a strong, vibrant beat of sexual energy,
And some that is soft and devotional.
Find music to evoke every kind of feeling:
Grief, longing, rage, joy, passion, and resentment.
Your compilation should be about thirty to forty-five minutes altogether.
Now, go to your room, switch off the phone, make sure you are undisturbed,
And play the music.
Enter into each of the feelings one by one.
You can dance; you can cry; you can call out in longing.
Use your whole body to express each feeling.
Make sounds.
Let the music guide you into each wave of feeling,
Free of any reason why.
When it is finished, lie down for several minutes and feel your body.

....

This is a quintessentially feminine practice. The feminine in all of us wants to feel without any restriction. It does not matter to the feminine heart if the feeling is so-called positive or negative; just the freedom to feel is enough. For the feminine, anything fully felt without limits is an easy portal back to the divine, back to love.

For millennia, the feminine has been dominated by the masculine's love of reason and logic. If you are sad, there must be a reason. If you are angry, there is something outside that made you so, and the solution is to find it and change it or fix it. As a result, we have been conditioned to always have a story, a reason for why we feel as we do.

Stories about why we think we have feelings turn them into soap operas and rob us of the possibility to feel them completely. When we are convinced that we know why we feel a certain way, then we become emotional and reactive. Now, I am angry with you because of what you did, and I want an apology and an explanation, and possibly revenge. All our energy goes into action and manipulation, and there is very little left for just *feeling*.

When we are really honest and pay careful attention to the fabric of our experience, we never really know for sure why we feel as we do. It is all made up. *Am I really angry because of what he said, or was it the driver who cut me off an hour before? Was it the cheap wine I had with dinner last night, or was it a memory from childhood, or even a past life?* We never really know for sure. Most of the time, if we can be really honest with ourselves, we can see that we already had the feeling before the event that we think caused it. We were angry before the insult; we were down before the rejection; we were giggly before the joke. It may well be the feeling which already existed that lassos that experience to us, giving rise to what we end up seeing as the cause.

This practice is an invitation to the feminine heart in all of us, to feel what arises free of any reason or story. It liberates feeling from the soap opera of why and because. You can do this practice alone, or a few people can get together and do this practice as a group. It takes longer than many of the other practices in this book, so you might not be able to do this every day. But just once a week will restore the capacity in you to feel unencumbered by logic, and this will overflow naturally into the rest of your life.

29

Explode with Anger

LEVEL OF DIFFICULTY ****

When you feel angry or resentful,

When you feel that some injustice has been done to you,

Stop and breathe deeply into the lower part of the belly.

Feel the energy there.

Feel the power.

Fill your lower belly with breath,

And let go of the story completely.

Every image, every explanation for why you feel as you do,

Let it all go. Let it be washed from you.

Stay with the raw energy in your belly.

You can place your hand there to help focus your attention.

Continue to bring the breath to this lower part of the belly,

And let it build and increase.

Build it up, more and more,

And let it explode in you.

If you need to make noise, growl like a lion.

If you are concerned about disturbing others, scream into
a cushion.

If you need to, you can beat and bite and throw the cushion.

Become pure anger itself, with no explanation, with no story.

Let it take over every part of your body.

Explode so completely that nothing is held back.

Then be still, lie down,

And feel the space inside.

Anger has a bad rap. This is unfortunate, as fully entering into anger can be one of the fastest and most dynamic ways to return to an open heart and an expansive consciousness. The two feelings that have been most repressed in organized society—by religion, governments, and schoolteachers alike—are anger and sexual arousal. You cannot control a population that is either angry or horny: in either state, they become uncontrollable. Because we have been conditioned to push anger down into the cells of the body, we have become terrified of our own anger, and hence the anger of the rest of the world at the same time. As a result, we are afraid that if we allow ourselves to feel anger, even for a moment, we might explode and become a serious danger to ourselves and to those close to us. We learn to keep anger behind a locked door by tightening our jaw muscles, constricting our diaphragm and our belly. With everything locked up in this way, not only do we prevent ourselves from feeling our anger, but we close off our love as well. Tragically, we cut ourselves off from the natural state of relaxed and open awareness.

The key to transforming anger from an obstacle to a blessing is letting go of the story of why we think we are angry. It is the conviction of this explanation in the mind that gives us justification for revenge, for violence, for throwing our anger out onto another. And truly, we can never really know its origin. We may come up with a million possible reasons why, but it is ultimately impossible to be sure of the source. You will never know, and you do not need to know.

If you can enter anger without any story, without any need to understand why, it will liberate you completely. Be generous with it; enjoy it fully, as much as you might enjoy having sex. You may feel ridiculous, to become angry without any reason or words—it's best to do this practice in private. Breathe fully, all the way down into the lower part of the belly. It can become a kind of cosmic orgasm. Five minutes of jumping into anger, alone, without any restraint, will deliver you into ecstatic release, into Oneness with all that is alive.

30

Enter Fear

LEVEL OF DIFFICULTY ****

When you notice yourself taken over by strong fear,
Enter it completely.
Use your fantasy to make the fear stronger,
But then let go of the story.
Remain in the midst of raw terror.
Look for where fear lives in the body,
And linger there with it.
Breathe softly and gently into the center of the fear.
With genuine curiosity, seek to discover the real nature of fear
When it is liberated from the stories told in the mind.
Stay patient with the fear until it opens its petals to you
And reveals its essence.
This is liberation from fear.

....

There is a beautiful Zen story, which I heard for the first time when I was a teenager, that transformed my relationship to fear ever since. A man was walking in the night by the side of a cliff, overlooking the ocean below. He lost his step, stumbled, and fell over the side of the cliff. He would have surely fallen to his death on the rocks several hundred feet below but for the fact that he grabbed on to a bush growing out of the side of the cliff. He clung to it for dear life. And so he stayed, for many, many hours. It was a dark night with no moon, and it was almost perfectly black. He could hear the waves crashing on the rocks below, and he knew that if he lost his grip, even for a moment, he would surely die. The whole night he remained like that, thinking only of the family he would leave behind, of all the things he had left undone. He was sure that sooner or later he would get too tired to hold on any more, or that he would fall asleep for a moment or two, and that would be the end of him. Finally, the dawn came, and there was enough light to see just a little bit. Below him, perhaps just eight or ten feet, was a narrow ledge, no more than three or four feet wide. At any time during the night, he could have let go, and he would have dropped to the ledge and rested there for the night.

Fear is created in the mind. You are almost never afraid of something that is real and here now: our fears are always of what might happen later. The only way to be free of fear is to face it completely, to use the taunting of the stories in the mind to take you into the essence of fear itself. And then the greatest joke of all reveals itself, all on its own, in the greatest release.

There is nothing to fear but fear itself.

31

Choose Depth over Pleasure

LEVEL OF DIFFICULTY ****

As you go about your day, notice the things you want for
yourself.
An ice cream. A coffee. A new gadget. Something new to wear.
Notice the things with which you become preoccupied.
Do they like me? How do I look? Are we there yet?
Stop to ask yourself:
In this moment now,
Am I pursuing fleeting pleasure,
Or am I seeking greater depth?
Whenever you ask yourself this question,
Discover how you could choose depth over pleasure,
Not only for yourself, but also for everyone around you.
Perhaps you still have the ice cream or the coffee,
Perhaps you choose again.
Perhaps you continue the gossip you have been involved in,
Perhaps you ask a deeper question.
For a few days,
Whenever you remember,
Choose depth over pleasure.

....

There is an old proverb in China. It was first told to me by an old
Chinese herbalist in San Francisco's Chinatown. He was trying
to persuade me to make a tea from herbs that smelled about as

bad as anything could ever smell. "That which tastes sweet in the beginning," he told me, "tastes bitter in the end. And that which tastes bitter in the beginning, tastes sweet in the end." He was not only talking about his herbs; he was equally talking about the ways that we distract ourselves with things that give us very little abiding nourishment.

To bring greater depth back to your life, to return to why you are alive and what gives you meaning and inspiration, does not take as much trouble as you might imagine. Sure, you could go on a retreat, take a trip to India or Nepal, or wait to have a religious epiphany. But this simple little practice can also transform the quality of the way that you live each day. So many of the things we think we want are not what we deeply long for at all, and do nothing to lead us there. And so much of what we long for, in the deepest caverns of the heart, we have forgotten even exists, or that we even have any right to ask for it. Give yourself permission to choose depth over pleasure, now and now and now.

You might be shy at first; you might feel pretentious or clumsy. "Deep" is so easy to make fun of—so "emo." Just passing time is so much safer. But this practice will grow on you. Start using it just once each day, in a small way. Perhaps you put down the magazine, close your eyes, and just feel for a moment. The next day you could try it twice. Each time you choose what really satisfies you, your confidence will grow, and you will find yourself inviting others into your adventure with you.

Section Six

Intimate
Relationship Practices

AN INTIMATE RELATIONSHIP CAN SOMETIMES seem like the greatest distraction to resting in the silence of our true nature. That is why, historically, the quest for the divine has often led to the cave or the monastery. But intimate relationships can equally be the greatest opportunity for genuine awakening. For self-realization, the meditation cushion may be ideal; to realize Oneness, however, it's necessary to practice in a relationship. Life *is* relationship.

We breathe the same air; we have the same thoughts, fears, and beliefs; we share the same visions and destiny. Rather than two separate entities meeting, a relationship becomes more like the waves in the ocean. On the surface, we appear to be two; as we move, we can come closer and farther apart. We can interact and experience one another. But when we look into ourselves, we discover that we are both just manifestations of the same ocean of Oneness. When a relationship is dedicated in this way, it becomes a temple no longer dedicated to desire but to Oneness.

The key to living a relationship as a practice is to become translucent: to be able to see oneself in the other, and as the other. This does not mean that when you look into your spouse's eyes you see your own personality, your own desires and fears. That would be a kind of delusion. It means that you know yourself to be deeper than that person you took yourself to be, with his or her story and distortions of perception. You know yourself to be space, free and open, with an infinite capacity to love, and the ability to recognize that the same mystery is looking back at you. The packaging may be a little different, but there you are, just the same. This is not a philosophical conclusion, but a direct perception.

32

Here-Nowing

LEVEL OF DIFFICULTY **

Stand facing your partner or a good friend.
Decide who will go first.
One of you will speak, and the other will receive.
Let your bodies be relaxed and comfortable,
Your arms hanging loosely by your sides,
Your legs relaxed so that your knees are not locked.
Look softly into one of your partner's eyes.
For the one receiving, you are going to be absolutely present.
Just looking, receiving, hearing, without any reaction at all.
You're going to be like the sky, open and receptive.
For the one speaking,
Looking into one of your partner's eyes,
Give a commentary on the present moment.
You're going to report on what is seen,
What is heard, what is felt in the body.
You can report on thoughts, on judgments, on memories.
But make sure you report them as thoughts.
Speak only of what is being experienced exactly now.
After five minutes, fall silent for a few seconds
And then switch roles.

....

My wife, Chameli, and I have done this practice together literally
thousands of times, over many years. This simple practice cultivates

two qualities, both of which are essential foundations for translucent relating.

The first essential quality is listening without reaction. When it is your turn to be receptive, keep absolutely still; do not react in any way. If your partner cracks a joke, do not laugh. If your partner starts to cry, you can be fully present in your heart, but do not interact in any way. Be like the open sky, receiving and being present for your partner in every way.

The other essential quality is that of radical honesty. You are learning to tell the truth about what is real in this moment without explanation, history, or blame. Absolute honesty means that the words coming from your lips are perfectly synchronized with the actuality of your moment-to-moment experience. Generally, when we try to be honest, we tell stories about the past: "I forgot to tell you that I never called to order the plane tickets." This is generally useful information, and a good thing to do. We would call that "sharing withholds," which we describe in practice 34. Radical honesty goes far beyond that. "I can see your eyes looking at me. I can feel the air entering my nostrils. I can hear the sound of the car passing outside." This is not useful information, and might get you wondering, What is the point?

This practice brings you both more deeply into the present moment, together. It quickly and effortlessly increases intimacy. When we can tell the truth about what is happening, now and now and now and now, without explanation or concept, we are revealed to be who we are behind the mask of reason: naked and absolutely innocent. "Here I am, like this. Take me or leave me; I am like this." In listening, we give our partner the greatest gift, the one that everyone is longing for: to be received unconditionally without evaluation, bypassing the conceptual mind.

Do this practice for five minutes, each way, every day at the same time for thirty days, and you will be amazed at the result. Do not do this practice when you are in crisis, but use it regularly and you will not enter crisis mode so easily.

33

Other Realization

LEVEL OF DIFFICULTY ****

Sit opposite someone close to you.

This could be your intimate partner, or a friend.

Look into each other's left eye.

Look not just at your partner's eye, but through the eye,

Into that which is looking back at you.

In this moment, something, someone is looking back at you.

What is that?

What is looking back through this eye and seeing you?

Stay present.

Keep the gaze with this left eye and keep inquiring,

Who am I meeting here?

Who is looking back at me?

What is it, who is it, I am meeting here?

Deeper than thoughts,

Deeper than feelings,

Who is this other?

....

Our usual habit is to feel everyone and everything as separate, and therefore to act and speak strategically. As long as we are held in the grip of separation, even when we are trying to be altruistic, we are still driven by the obsession with "me": *How do I fulfill* my *needs? What am* I *feeling? How can I express* my *truth?* It is, in fact, this underlying feeling of separation that causes us suffering in relationships, more than who said or did what to whom.

When we relate to each other from a place of separation, we act as if the other person is on the far side of a deep canyon. We can shout and wave and find empathy in our feelings of isolation. So-called "skillful communication" means building a stable and well-constructed bridge between one side and another to effect transactions. But even then, the deep feeling of isolation has not been addressed.

The trance of separation begins to be broken only when we inquire into our own nature. Where we might have thought there was a person, we begin to discover spaciousness, presence, pure awareness itself. This is called self-realization, and it may come all at once, in a flash out of nowhere, or it may creep up on you in ever-increasing intensity.

You can also look into the eyes of another and discover who is looking back at you. We need to look beyond the appearance of a face, a name, and an agenda, and find out who is really there, behind those eyes, seeing you. When this inquiry extends to another person, we can call it "other realization." We start by finding infinity within our own heart, but soon that discovering expands to everyone around us.

To recognize that the one behind your own eyes and the one behind the other's eyes are the same is love. Practice often in this way. It overflows to all things, to Oneness with all life: the realization that I am the tree, I am the ant, I am the saint, and I am the criminal. Underneath all our desires, our structures, our hopes and dreams, the deepest longing of the heart is for Oneness, absolute intimacy with all that is. Experiment for yourself with innocence and sincerity, looking deeply into the face of another, and find out if this is true.

34

Share Witholds

LEVEL OF DIFFICULTY ***

Sit together with your intimate partner or a close friend.

Decide who will be partner A, and who will be B.

Partner A, you are going to share five withholds:

Something significant and relevant to your relationship

That has not been said.

This could be a judgment, it could be something that happened,

Or it could be something you have been thinking or planning.

Keep your withholds short: no more than a sentence or two.

Partner B, after each withhold, just say "thank you."

Do not respond or react in any other way.

After five withholds, close your eyes and sit together for a few minutes,

Then switch roles.

....

Gay and Kathlyn Hendricks talk about relationship like a dance floor. You are moving together, coming very close and then moving away for a moment, moving fast and then slow. Your relationship is set to different kinds of music with different tempos, and the tempo can change at any time. At any moment, you both need to be ready and available to respond to the change in the rhythm or the speed of the dance. They describe withheld communication as globs of chewing gum on the dance floor, where your shoes get stuck. The dance can no longer flow.

We may have all kinds of motivations in our life to be honest or dishonest. Here, we are using it as a practice not for the usual moral or strategic reasons, but to create more space for the dance to flow. When we share and dissolve our withholds in this way, we let go of the boundaries that keep us separate.

This practice is less about the exchange of information than it is about a spirit of self-effacing disclosure. The withholds you share may seem very significant and important: "I'm considering moving to Canada." "I slept with your sister." "Yesterday when you said what you did in the restaurant, I felt really hurt." Or they might seem quite petty and mundane, not even worth mentioning: "I don't like the color of your socks." "Your stories bore me." "I had a cigarette yesterday, after I said I had quit." Keep them very short: label and move on. We are not psychologically processing here, but letting go of what gets in the way. Once it has been said, it is done.

When you are the one listening, it is important not to react in any way. Just listen and breathe and let go. Don't throw things back in your partner's face by making one of your withholds be a reaction to what was just said. After you are both done, there should be no postmortem, no discussion of what was said. This may sound difficult, but it doesn't take long to recognize the great value of this of this practice.

When we tell the truth about something, we open the door to a deeper intimacy with the other person. We create and share more space. Share your withholds often, so they do not build up.

Enjoy the greater space you open between you, and within you.

35

Listen with All of You

LEVEL OF DIFFICULTY ***

When your partner or anyone close to you is speaking to you,
Whether telling you a story, lodging a complaint, or sharing a
feeling,
Give your undivided attention.
Listen with all of you:
With your ears, with your heart, with your skin, with your
breath.
Pay attention so completely that everything else disappears.
Listen not only to the words,
But to the mysterious presence from which those words arise.
Listen to the sound of the voice, to the inflections.
Listen to the silence between the words.
Listen to what was not said, but can still be sensed.
In giving absolute attention,
Become the beloved for which the heart has always longed.
Be available in this way for as long as is practical.
Then give love and blessings
And move on with your day.
Whenever you are able to listen,
Listen with all of you.

....

We live in a multitasking nation. We cook while we talk while we
have an ear out for what's on the news. We drive while we check

messages on the cell phone while we mumble perfunctory grunts to what someone is telling us. The most you can hope to receive when you are half-listening is information. Then, when the other person accuses you of not really being there, you can conveniently say, "Yes I am. You just told me that you went shopping today, and you bought avocados." You are off the hook; the charges are dropped; the trial is acquitted. But that acquittal is a booby prize. Everyone loses. Real communication is abandoned.

This way of spreading attention over a wide array of stimuli is a primary cause of stress, and also deprives us of being fully satisfied by any of it. As we slide through interactions by making the correct kinds of grunting sounds at the right time, we also deprive those speaking to us of what they most crave: full attention.

When you listen completely, with nothing else going on, it becomes more than listening. If you give your full attention, the person before you becomes fascinating, multidimensional, no matter how mundane his or her topic may be. When you stop everything and bring yourself fully to another person, a little bit will go a long way. This is what everyone is longing for: it is immensely nourishing to be fully received, even for a few minutes at a time.

You do not need to do this practice all the time in order for it to bring huge benefit not only to you as the listener, but to the person speaking to you also. If you are not immediately available, ask for a few minutes. Then listen with totality: five or ten minutes will often be enough.

In this, everyone moves closer to Oneness.

36

Exchange Points of View

LEVEL OF DIFFICULTY ****

When you find yourself caught in a disagreement
With your partner or a close friend,
When you are arguing,
Trying to be convincing that your point of view is more correct,
Stop and exchange points of view.
If you have been sitting together and talking,
Stand up and change seats.
For five minutes, you will represent the point of view
of the other,
Vehemently, passionately, fully trying to convince.
Do this with totality; give it everything.
Make sure you include (as the other)
How you feel, what you're resentful about,
What you want and why,
And what you are afraid of.
After doing this exercise for five minutes
Move back to your original position,
Take the point of view that was originally yours,
And see what remains of your dispute.

....

Sometimes, needing to be right eclipses what is really right: that which will serve the greatest good. We get attached to a position like an old jacket full of holes that lets the water in; it no longer serves us but is comfortable and habitual. And so it is that the positions we take become prisons of our own creating; we isolate ourselves with our own fundamentalism.

In order for this practice to really help you, it is important to do it with totality and sincerity. Really deeply *become* the other person, so you can feel their hurts, their ambitions, their unfulfilled dreams. Don't imitate; become. It takes presence and the willingness to let go of your own view in order really feel what another is feeling.

You might need to switch back and forth a few times to get the hang of this. You and your partner will need a shared commitment to step beyond your mutual need to be right, a willingness to let go of all positions. The key is not only to do this through the mind, but also through the body. As well as taking on the beliefs and thoughts of your partner, when you exchange positions you can also feel what it is like to have this body, to have this particular set of tensions and energies. It is through *feeling* what it is like to be the other, more than thinking as the other, that you will move more deeply into Oneness.

The point of this practice is not to win the war or to lose it, nor even to negotiate a compromise, but to feel what remains when the very basis of conflict is removed. You may find that underneath and including both these points of view rests what is right, what is best for all concerned.

37

Become the Other

LEVEL OF DIFFICULTY ****

When you find yourself courting conflict with another person,

Go somewhere alone where you can be undisturbed.

Put two cushions down on the bed or the floor.

Sit on one of them, and close your eyes.

Imagine the other person is sitting before you on the other cushion.

What is this other wearing? How is their hair?

What is the expression on their face?

Let yourself see their eyes and hear their voice.

Now, speak out loud to them for about a minute.

Tell the other everything that has been held back. Be total.

Now, stop, and listen.

Listen to what the other has to say to you.

After another minute, again speak.

Fueled by what you have heard, say everything.

Be as open and vulnerable and truthful as you can.

Now get up from your cushion,

Move over and sit down on the cushion of the other.

Let yourself completely become this other person,

Not just imagining what they would say, but really feeling what they feel.

Notice what it is like to have these thoughts, these feelings,

These body sensations, to have this body itself.

Speak completely as this other person,

Say everything that has been held back.

After another minute, get up and move back to your original cushion.

Slip back into being yourself as though you were putting on a T-shirt, and speak again.

Finally, stand up.

Stand between the cushions,

So one identity is on your left and one is on your right.

Extend your arms out,

And feel both of these identities embraced here.

Take a breath and welcome them both into your heart.

....

I have shared this simple practice in workshops with thousands of people over many years. I'm still amazed by how often people come back to me and say that after they themselves did this practice, it was the other person who changed! For example, there was a man in a seminar who had once been married for several years. They were both young and, as far as he was concerned, they were both very much in love. One day he got home, and his wife was gone. She had left a note saying that things were too much for her, and she was leaving. Since then, the man had never heard from her. He got married again, but he could never be fully in the relationship; he was holding on to too much hurt from what had happened. He did this simple practice. He placed his wife from many years before on the cushion in front of him, and spoke to her. He told her of his pain, his feelings of abandonment. He listened to her, and then he spoke again. But it was only when he switched his body over and became his young wife from that time that the transformation happened. He felt in his body her feeling of entrapment, her inability to communicate with him, her despair. He felt in his own body the panic that led her to her desperate flight. After the workshop was over, when he arrived home, there was a message on his machine. "I know you must be surprised to hear from me after all these years. I did not even have your number. I had to get it from the directory. I would love to talk with you." A few days later, he met with his ex-wife, and they passed through a deep resolution and healing. He was able to fully let go, and his present marriage became much richer as a result.

You can do this practice with someone who is on the other side of the earth. You can do it with someone who is estranged, with whom you have no contact. You can do this with someone who is no longer alive. This practice opens to you the reality that nothing is truly separate from anything or anyone else. You can know and feel completely what another person is feeling and thinking, what they want, what they regret. The purpose of this practice is not to achieve any particular result, although that may happen. The aim is not to be right, or to get your own way, but rather to dissolve the feeling of the me and the not-me.

38

Give What You Hope to Receive

LEVEL OF DIFFICULTY ****

When you notice yourself wanting something from your
partner,
Stop and label it.
I need your respect;
I need you to clean up after yourself;
I need you to notice how much I do for you.
Once you become aware of the need for certain qualities
in this way,
Give what you hope to receive.
If you are demanding respect from your partner,
Give your partner respect.
If you are demanding to be heard by your partner,
Make a practice of hearing.
If you are demanding that your partner be more mindful,
Try to pay closer attention to each moment.
Shift the attention from the trickle
You hope to elicit from outside,
To the ocean that you can become within yourself.

....

Relationships so easily become a negotiation of trying to get our
needs met. Good luck. Perhaps you have noticed how frustrating
it can be to try to change another person, to make them give you
what you think you want. When you start to do this practice,

you may notice that your longing is for a certain quality as much as for a practical external change; in that recognition, you can become that quality within yourself.

Of course, if this is the only practice that you and your partner do, it could easily become problematic. So use the wise council of your friends and family to consider if this is a practice that could support you. It can be so helpful for anyone who is in the habit of trying to get things from the outside, and criticizing and complaining when it doesn't happen. In such a situation, shifting the attention more to oneself, to all the gifts that have accumulated and remained ungiven, can have enormous benefit.

Use this practice to shift from trying to manipulate reality to discovering the treasures hidden in your own heart. Many people discover that when they are willing to embody what they have tried to get from the outside, the outer world cooperates. When you become the kindness you were demanding, the world becomes a kinder place.

If you have a habit of taking care of everyone else before yourself and putting your own needs last, this would not be the right practice for you; you would benefit more from the practices in the meditation or feelings sections to nurture yourself more.

39

Welcome Criticism

LEVEL OF DIFFICULTY *****

When your partner or someone close to you

Criticizes you in any way,

Relax and welcome it.

At times like this it is natural to feel defensive,

To want to argue,

To think of rationalizing why it is not true.

But just listen.

Find the elements in what is said,

Where there is some truth in it, and stay with that.

Take it as a gift.

Thank your friend for supporting you in living with greater
freedom.

Practice in this way just long enough to hear the essence of the
criticism.

Don't linger on it so that it becomes masochistic.

When you have heard the criticism

And digested the essence of it,

Thank your partner,

Bow,

And be complete.

....

The habitual response to being criticized is to defend and rational-
ize. If we feel under attack, it is natural to want to protect ourselves.

Of course, if someone is repeatedly critical without any balance of support and love, it becomes a toxic relationship, and it is only intelligent to take some space for oneself.

But many times when we are criticized by those close to us, there is a great jewel that we miss completely when we defend ourselves. Even when someone is in a bad mood, or tired or irritated, you can often feel deeper than that mood, to the gift they are trying to give you. What can be seen as destructive criticism can also be received as loving and constructive feedback. The difference is not so much in their communication but in how you receive it. Somewhere in their heart, they want to support you to go to a deeper place.

When you can receive criticism with gratitude, when you can receive it as a gift, you will be amazed how quickly things can change. First of all, when you have the intention to feel the other person's highest wishes and caring for you, your heart will open and flower. The habitual reactive contractions won't take over. The world will seem like a more friendly place. Second, the other person will also relax and soften and become more calm. If you receive what they are saying with grace and gratitude, the charge behind it will quickly melt away, because there is nothing to push against. That person now feels received and heard, which is what everyone is most deeply longing for in their heart of hearts.

When you practice receiving criticism in this way without argument, without defense, seeking out what is true in what is being said, you will both feel blessed.

40

Celebrate Dependency

LEVEL OF DIFFICULTY ****

When you start to feel needy or insecure,
Celebrate it completely.
Ask your partner to sit in a chair or on the sofa,
And sit at your partner's feet for a few minutes.
Enter into your fear of abandonment,
The need to be loved completely.
Don't leave me. Don't leave me. I beg you.
I need you so much.
I can't live without you. Please stay with me.
Look at me. Look at me. I want you. I need you.
Please don't leave me.
As you enter more fully into this practice,
It will overflow from this exploration into deeper feeling.
You may find yourself crying.
It may evoke long-forgotten memories in you,
Or even the call of the heart to the divine.
If you are the one sitting in the chair or on the sofa
Do not react in any way.
Above all do not try to reassure or comfort your partner.
But equally do not reject him or her.
Just look and experience your partner without reaction.
Do this practice for about five minutes,
Then stand up, shake, and let it go.
If you choose to, you can reverse roles

Many couples find it helpful to do this practice every day for
a month
And then stop.

....

Any feeling you resist will eventually become ugly and something
you feel ashamed of. If you repress sex, it becomes perversion. If
you repress anger, it becomes bitterness and tension. If you repress
neediness, it becomes aloofness and distance. The dilemma we all
get caught in is whether to repress our feelings to try to keep a
good façade, or to act them out and risk alienating other people
by being "too much." This is true more than ever with the feeling
of neediness. If we show signs of being dependent and clingy, we
are afraid that we will become ugly and repulsive to our partner,
especially if the relationship is new.

The way to transcend this dilemma is through transforming
neurosis into art. You can turn any feeling you might otherwise
be ashamed of into an art form when you introduce an element of
awareness and conscious choice and, even more important, a sense
of humor. Whatever is celebrated in this way, neediness, jealousy,
control, or criticism, becomes a form of entertainment.

Why do people enjoy the films of Woody Allen so much, or
Rowan Atkinson? The same personality traits they exhibit could
be painful to watch if they were hidden and repressed, but by being celebrated and slightly exaggerated, they are transformed into
an art form.

When neediness is celebrated in this way, you will actually come
to enjoy it. It is a relief to let it pour out; in your totality you will

feel passion, tremendous aliveness. And your partner will enjoy it also: neediness can be sexy, funny, and energizing when it is celebrated as a work of art.

Section Seven

Sex Practices

ANOTHER POWERFUL REALM OF PRACTICE is our sexual life. Sexual meeting is probably the most directly powerful energetic event that we know. Our whole culture is obsessed with sexuality. Why? Because when we are taken over, even to a small extent, by the sexual energy in the body, we go out of the mind. We become less conceptual, less interested in past and future. We become more aware of our bodies, and we feel more alive. Sex is very often used as a destination. We rub the body in the right way when we need a release of some kind, an energetic explosion. But sex can also be a doorway into divinity, not simply into release but into endless opening.

The physical act of sex can be an end in itself or a take-off point for a more embodied and awakened life. There are so many dimensions to who we are, and they are all real. In one sense, you and your partner are both animals who evolved out of basic biological needs, basic biological urges. In another dimension, you and your partner are complex psyches. We have all kinds of unmet needs and buried hurts, and sex can easily become a way for those to enact themselves. Through practice, you and your partner can also discover in glimpses that you have the capacity to return back to your basic natural presence. Because it is such a strong energy, sex can be the most powerful way to return to that place. But don't try to make every event of lovemaking into a sacred act: it will quickly become shallow if you do. You can create agreements with your partner to explore all of the different aspects of sexual energy when you make love. The practices in this section are just a beginning, but they will give you a small hint of what is possible to explore and discover in this way.

41

Be Still in Sex

LEVEL OF DIFFICULTY ***

Lie down naked with your partner,
Making sure you will be undisturbed for some time.
Begin to enjoy caressing each other,
And slowly move into making love.
Sexual arousal comes in waves.
Wait until you feel turned on,
Until your breath has quickened,
Until you feel pulled to be taken over by passion.
When it has reached this intensity,
Stop. Be still, and feel.
Allow your attention to be with your whole body,
Even to feel through your body into your partner.
Look into your partner's eyes, and be still.
Breathe down into your genitals.
Flood the genital area with your in-breath.
Let the sexual energy that has built up
Spread into the rest of your pelvis,
Spread up through the spine into the rest of the body.
In this stillness in the midst of passion,
Find the essence of all mysteries.

....

Sex can be so many things. We have all entered into sex as a quick release, a vehicle for pent-up emotion. When sex is driven only by immediate desire and passion, the energy builds up, and we crave release. This kind of explosion can certainly be pleasurable, and it is good for this to happen between you sometimes.

However, sex can also be the catalyst that creates a deeper love. Only then can we rightly call it "making love." To allow sex to become a portal to the divine will require us to shift from merely getting lost in sensation and emotion to a dedication to this present moment, a willingness to feel without limits. We can make sex into a sacred spiritual discipline. This practice will give you another way to experience sex, wherein the buildup of desire and pleasure is no longer an end in itself, but the beginning of a much greater expansion.

Most people enter lovemaking with clear expectations of getting something from the other person, and often we follow a habitual routine. If you take on this practice, it allows a space for something new to happen. Every time you stop and disrupt the familiar patterns of how you make love, you are both thrown into the unknown. Then, you simply have to wait for an impulse from the body to know when and where to move. If you have trouble staying present, you may choose to maintain a commentary on everything you are feeling, both physical sensations and emotions. You can alternate your lovemaking between enjoying the animal lust of the body and moving into this more expansive plateau of intimacy. If you practice often this way, your capacity to experience pleasure, opening through your whole body, will increase every time.

42

Sex as Worship

LEVEL OF DIFFICULTY ***

Make a date with your beloved for sacred sex.

Prepare the room like a temple:

Incense, candles, rose petals, and soft colors.

Choose music that evokes devotion more than passion.

Prepare yourself. Wash your body.

Dress as if you were meeting God.

Approach each other with respect,

With worship.

Bow to your beloved.

Let this whole process be slow and delicate,

With absolute respect and sacredness.

Touch not with desire, but with worship,

As if you were touching a deity.

When you make love, feel this as the most blessed moment.

In this way, allow yourself

To make love with the divine.

....

To transform sex from an act of lust to a ritual of worship, all that is needed is to approach your partner in a different way. It requires a decision. Often we bring this spirit of worship to lovemaking when we are first in a relationship. We call it being in love, and we see the beloved with the eyes of the devotee. With time, familiarity causes it to wane, and it is possible to take your beloved for granted. It is the same person you once fell in love with, but now see through tired eyes.

You can bring the sacredness back at any time. If you are willing to see your partner in a fresh way, the magic is immediately restored. You could begin the practice with the "Couples Puja" (practice 61), or by sitting silently together. Throughout this practice, speak the language of worship and devotion: tell your partner how beautiful he or she is, express the feelings evoked in you. Go very slowly, almost in slow motion, with no end goal in mind.

This kind of lovemaking doesn't need to finish in orgasm. In fact, bringing this spirit to lovemaking may bypass the need for orgasm altogether. There will come a time when you both feel full and complete. When you know that you've come to the conclusion, respectfully and gently disengage your bodies and bow to each other in gratitude.

It is best not to dedicate every lovemaking in this way, for it loses its specialness. Alternate it with times when you can simply enjoy your passion. Make a date many days in advance to practice in this way, so it is not tied to fleeting desire or passion but to a conscious decision to create sacred space.

43

For Men: Bring the Energy Up the Spine

LEVEL OF DIFFICULTY ****

Begin this practice alone.

Stimulate your penis until you become erect.

Long before you feel the need to ejaculate,

You will start to feel the buildup of energy

In the head of your penis.

As soon as you begin to feel it,

Use your in-breath to draw the energy first into the perineum

(halfway between the base of the penis and the rectum)

And then gradually up the spine,

As if you are drawing liquid up through a straw.

You can draw the energy up

With one long in-breath through the nose

Or with a series of deep, sharp sniffs.

If you lose energy in the penis,

Stimulate yourself again, just enough until the energy

begins to build.

Practice in this way alone for about twenty to thirty minutes.

After you become proficient

You can bring this practice to your lovemaking with

your partner.

....

The ancient Taoist masters discovered many things about the relationship between sex, the health of the body, and the embodiment of awakened consciousness. This simple practice affects all three.

First, when sexual energy stays trapped in the genitals, it cannot build up much without the need for release and ejaculation. For a man, it is more difficult to bring a woman beyond her limits and into ecstatic flow if this is the case. So, in addition to prolonging the experience for yourself, this practice will make you a deeper and more generous lover.

Second, it is said in both Ayurveda and Taoist medicine that the semen is the quintessential peak of the digestive process. The very best of what the body can produce becomes the semen; it contains the seed of new life. According to these traditions, if this elixir of the body is lost frequently, it will result in weakness, lack of energy, and even depression. When the *ojas* (life essence) accumulated in the testicles builds up and spreads to the rest of the body, it can rejuvenate and restore every part of the body. The Taoist masters who practiced in this way are reported to have lived sometimes in perfect health into their nineties and beyond.

Third, as the vital energy spreads up the spine through all the organs, it reaches to the crown of the head and becomes radiant presence—the essence of meditation.

In the beginning, you may only feel this practice in a fairly mild and localized way. You may only feel a subtle shift from the head of the penis, or you may feel no shift at all. Be patient; as you practice, you will find that each time you can draw the energy up to a certain point in the spine. This becomes a benchmark for you every time, and you can start from there the next time. Eventually, it will reach up into the belly and flood the organs with life force, spreading through all the energetic centers in the spine—the chakras—and, finally, to the top of the head.

Through this practice, you will discover the huge difference between orgasm and ejaculation. You can have an orgasm in the heart, in the belly, in the throat, or even in the third eye. An orgasm in the genitals is generally accompanied by the release of semen, but an orgasm in the heart will be felt as an explosion of love; an orgasm in the belly may be felt as an explosion of pure power.

Once you master this practice, you can bring it to your partner also. You can begin to make love in the normal way, but once you feel the energy building, you can use your breath to draw the sexual energy up into the rest of the body also. You can give the gift of your love in a much deeper way to your partner, not only through your genitals but with your whole body. The ultimate way to give to each other is in Oneness, where the giver and the gifted are the same. This begins with bringing your whole body to your partner.

Please be aware that this practice can be very powerful and can have strong effects on the energetic balance of your whole system. Although these pages have been an introduction to the possibilities, before diving in more deeply please consult a book or teaching that can take you deeper, such as *The Multi-Orgasmic Man* by Mantak Chia.

44

For Women: Radiate Love from Your Breasts

LEVEL OF DIFFICULTY ***

Find a quiet place where you can be alone.
Bring your whole attention to the breasts.
You can touch them, massage them,
Breathe softly into them,
And feel them as radiant light.
Lie down on your back.
With every in-breath, raise the small of your back,
Tilting your pelvis downward,
And fill your chest and breasts with life.
With every out-breath,
Feel your breasts radiating as light.
You can start by imagining a light that shines
From your breasts into the room where you are.
You can allow that light to spread
From your breasts to the whole area around you.
Finally, you can reach out to every sentient being
With the radiant light of the love
Flowing from your breasts.

....

In the yogic and Buddhist Tantric traditions that have developed in India, it is said that the masculine and feminine bodies are half circuits. The masculine body has a positive or excess charge of energy in the penis, but a negative charge in the chest. The feminine body has a negative or receptive charge in the genital area, and a positive or excess charge in the breasts.

As a woman, if you just breathe into your breasts, even for a few moments, you will feel you body immediately transformed. You will feel lighter, more radiant, more compassionate and embracing. You will start to feel a motherly energy flow into everything you see. Try it on the bus or the train, focusing your energy in the breasts for just a few moments, and see what happens. You will start to feel a divine mothering energy for total strangers; you will want to embrace everyone.

This practice amplifies the natural tendency to feel love through the breasts. If you can, move more deeply into this practice; lie down in an undisturbed way for twenty minutes or longer. Imagine that you are being made love to, that you are being penetrated by the divine. Call on the divine force to enter you. As you breathe in, draw this energy up into your breasts, and on the out-breath radiate it out through the breasts as limitless love.

During this practice, you might feel some pain, either physical or emotional, in the breasts. Keep breathing through it. As you draw more of this love through your breasts, it will also heal the breasts themselves.

Finally, you can bring this practice to your lovemaking. If you are heterosexual, when your partner penetrates you, draw the positively charged energy from his penis through your vagina and up into the breasts. Give everything to your partner through your breasts: your love, your gratitude, your devotion. Fill his chest with your love. This charge of energy into his chest will naturally bring more energy into his penis, and so the cycle will build and grow.

We often guide gay couples in these practices as well. Even though you are both the same gender, there is still a play of masculine and feminine polarities, which may alternate between you. Through openhearted experimenting, you will discover how you can bring translucent practice to your lovemaking.

45

Make Love to Everything

LEVEL OF DIFFICULTY ****

While in the midst of making love,
Feel your partner completely.
Be absolutely present with your beloved.
Stay with your beloved,
And let your attention expand.
Include your beloved and what is beyond,
Everything around you.
Feel that you are making love with that, too.
Let it expand even more.
Let it keep expanding,
Until you're making love with the trees outside the window.
You're making love to more and more of life.
Keep breathing and expanding
Until you are making love with everything.
This practice can continue
After physical sex has come to a completion.

....

For most of us, making love starts in a sexual relationship, in a private exchange of physical pleasure. And certainly for almost everyone, that turns out to be the best way to experience sexual energy: in a monogamous relationship. But making love can expand beyond sex. Your participation in just about everything can become a form of lovemaking. The sexual lovemaking you share with your partner can become a catalyst to support yourself and your partner in pouring forth your love in many other ways. Parenting can be a kind of lovemaking. Business, serving your community or the planet, making a home beautiful—these are not sexual activities, but they can certainly be forms of lovemaking, and they can certainly be orgasmic.

If your partner were to explore sexuality outside of your relationship, you would probably feel jealous, contracted, and betrayed. But imagine that you make love with your partner, and you both feel your hearts more open, and more deeply present. Imagine that your partner were moved to share that gift of an open heart, of a deeper presence, in his or her participation in the rest of life, of course without any sexual energy involved. Imagine that your lovemaking caused your partner to be kinder with the children, more creative at work, or more inspired to make a difference in the world at large. You would more than likely feel expanded. You would more than likely feel that you have supported each other in becoming more authentically yourselves in awakening the gift that you were born to live.

This does not mean that you will behave in an overtly sexual or flirtatious way, but that when you move into the rest of the day you will meet life with a disposition of openness. For a man, you can still feel that you are making love to the feminine everywhere. Your decisions, your acts of service, become a way of penetrating life with your presence. For a woman, you can allow yourself to feel the divine force that is everywhere, entering you, waking up the energy in your pelvis, and you can continue to draw it up into your heart and to give love and blessings to everything around you. If you do this practice with totality, everyone around you will simply feel you to be absolutely present and loving, a gift to all of life.

Section Eight

Family Practices

ANOTHER RICH REALM OF PRACTICE is with our families. There's an old assumption that family life is so full of attachment and distraction that you must choose, just as the Buddha did, between family and the pursuit of liberation. Today, people are discovering that family itself, our connection with our children, siblings, parents, and extended family, can be a path to discovering Oneness.

The relationship we have with our children, particularly when they are very young, is not one of give and take. It is give and give. Just like many of the other translucent practices in this book, being a parent expands us beyond what we thought were the outer limits of our capacity to give. Whether or not you think you have had a radical awakening, whether or not you define yourself as a spiritual person or just a regular slob, it is as a parent that you generally have the most vivid glimpses of your translucent potential.

When we are willing to approach parenting as a spiritual practice, we are at first faced with all the hardwired assumptions that have been passed on to us from previous generations: what it means to be a good parent, the dos and don'ts and shoulds and shouldn'ts of raising a child. Our notions of parenting are either carbon copies of how we were parented, or rebellious reactions against it. To the degree that we can question those beliefs, we are able to enter parenting as a process of learning, rather than simply asserting that we know what is best, or at least faking it.

Once we can meet our children, even for moments, in a spirit of "I don't know," of relinquished authority, we return to the realms of mystery and magic, where real connection becomes alive again. Without the need to be right about everything, we can meet our children in a relationship of mutuality and respect. As parents, we can demonstrate an openness to learning and a surrender rather than demanding obedience from our children as an unquestioned right. We can certainly teach our children about the material world, about things that are not obvious or intuitive. The mutuality comes in the recognition that there are also many things our children can teach us, or at least remind us of—things we have forgotten. For example, my children teach me a great deal about integrity, about keeping my word. They always notice when I say I'll do things and then don't follow through. They point it out to me, not always logically, but it always makes the point.

46

Rotate the Boss in Your Family

LEVEL OF DIFFICULTY ***

Every now and then,

Once a week or so,

When something needs to be done,

Such as cleaning the house, working in the garden,

Or making a meal,

Get the whole family together.

Make a list of what needs to be done, and how long it will take.

Divide the time among everyone present:

Two hours cleaning for four people means half an hour each.

Everyone gets a turn to be the boss,

From the youngest to the oldest.

When it is your turn to rule,

Be a benevolent and loving dictator.

Your word is law.

When it is not your turn,

Surrender completely.

Discover a new world.

....

We started this game in our family many years ago when Shuba, my youngest son, was only seven. The designated cleaning day was Saturday, and every time it came around, Shuba would move into resistance, the adults in the family would become dictatorial and easily frustrated, and Abhi, my oldest son, would try to avoid the situation altogether. Then we had the idea of rotating the role of the boss. We resented having all the responsibility, and Shuba resented being told what to do all the time, so the best thing seemed to be a switch. We agreed that everyone would get to be the boss for half an hour, starting out with Shuba. For the first half hour, he would be the king, would allocate the jobs, supervise that they were getting done correctly, and tell the rest of us when to move on to a new one.

You might anticipate, as we did, that this would be chaos—that Shuba might give crazy commands or not know what to do and fall apart. But it was not like that at all. He turned out to be the most caring and careful supervisor in the whole family. He was attentive to detail, but equally as attentive to the needs of the person cleaning. "Do you have everything you need? Are you clear about what to do? Let me know if you need a break." I was amazed; this was a complete personality transformation. As soon as his half hour was up, of course, he resorted to his usual personality, complaining bitterly about all the work he had to do.

Of course, we cannot do this every day. Kids need to be kids, and to have fun and freedom from responsibility. And generally, adults need to make the decisions about what to eat and when to sleep and when to leave for school. But every now and then, shaking up our family roles and responsibilities loosens our encrusted habits, and gives everyone an opportunity to find greater space and freedom within themselves.

47

Exchange Personalities over Dinner

LEVEL OF DIFFICULTY **

Over family dinner,
With your spouse and children,
Or your parents and siblings
Or even a group of your friends,
Swap personalities among yourselves.
Have everyone write their name down on a small piece
of paper,
And place all the names in a bowl.
Mix them up, and have everyone pick a name.
For five minutes, you will become that person completely,
Not as a caricature, but with totality.
Feel what it is like to have their body, their feelings,
their thoughts.
Relate to the others at the table authentically from this place.
If you get your own name, take on your own personality
As if for the first time.
After five minutes, you can switch,
Until you have all become everyone else at the table.

....

A family can be a place of confinement or of liberation. Many of us have come to see the dynamics within the family as restrictive, habits of restraint handed down from one generation to the next, and so we come to see our kin as the opposite of freedom.

Fortunately, it does not take much to reverse that and allow those closest to us to become our allies in freedom.

Families become restrictive to the degree that everyone is allocated a strict role to which they must conform. "Go wash your hands." "Why, Mummy?" "Because I say so." She says it with tension in her voice, like she is about to burst. The teenage son rolls his eyes at the ceiling. The father glances at his BlackBerry, hoping it will not be noticed. Even our pets go on automatic pilot. Everyone ends up living in a small and well-defined box. A parent is expected to be responsible, serious, hardworking, and at times, dictatorial. The youngest child is cute, adoring, carefree, sometimes irresponsible. The oldest child is expected to be independent, a leader, and to sometimes reject authority.

These are all roles we perform, and they can easily be confused with who we really are. As soon as you slip out of the automation of the role, however, even for just a moment, there is an explosion of freedom and creativity that is suddenly available. The youngest child also has the seeds of parenthood: just see her with her dolls or a puppy. The mother carries with her still the seeds of carefree enjoyment: just look at her on the rare vacation without the kids.

It does not take much to reverse all that, to allow those closest to us to become our allies in freedom. Slip out of your tight role as you might pull a T-shirt over your head. Pass the roles around. You will expand beyond who you thought you were, and laugh out loud at the same time.

48

Chant on the Way to School

> Driving on the way to school,
> Or whenever you are all together as a family
> With nothing else to do,
> Chant or sing together.
> Say the words together out loud a few times
> Until everyone can remember them,
> Then sing the chant over and over together.
> You can use mantras from India,
> Chants from the Native American elders,
> Hymns from the Christian tradition,
> Or Sufi songs from Persia.
> Repeat the same chants every day.
> In chanting together, you become as one.

. . . .

Chanting is one of the most ancient of practices for bringing us directly into the flowering of the heart, into the now. Chanting mantras and singing hymns have been used in every spiritual tradition throughout the world for as long as we can remember. Certain sounds carry deep imprints of awakening. One of my favorites is the Gayatri mantra, which many scholars say is the oldest mantra known to man. It is said that in India there has always been someone, somewhere, chanting this mantra for more than five thousand years. It is not a religious chant as much as a wish for all beings to awaken to the truth and to be free.

Om bhur bhuva swaha
Tat savetur varenyam
Bhargo devasya dheemahi
Dhiyo yon aha prachodayat

(Great creative force, the giver of all life, the remover of pain and sorrow, the bestower of happiness, shining brightly like the sun: may we all receive the supreme light which dispels darkness, and may the supreme intelligence guide us in the bright direction of awakening.)

There is a wonderful version of this ancient mantra on Deva Premal's album *The Essence,* with a beautiful melody that is easy for everyone to sing. When you sing ancient mantras like this, you quickly become one with the sound itself and forget your preoccupations and self-involvement. After you are done, there is a whole new feeling among all of you: you will simply feel more connection, more Oneness.

You might wonder how to persuade teenage children to chant mantras. I have found a simple solution: we make a deal. You chant Gayatri mantra with me, and then we'll switch on your favorite station: KRQR, The Rocker.

49

Give Appreciation

LEVEL OF DIFFICULTY **

Sit together with your family
And express your appreciation for each other.
You can do this in rounds.
Start with anyone.
Dad, I really appreciate that you drive us everywhere.
Milly, I really appreciate how kind you are to your cat.
Mom, I appreciate that you make sure we eat good food.
Continue the round, until everyone gives appreciation to one
other person.
Then do a second round, and a third,
Until everyone has appreciated everyone else in the family.
Do this every day for at least a week
When you are all in the car,
Or eating a meal.
Notice not only how it makes people feel to be appreciated,
But how it feels in you to give appreciation.

....

Often in a family we only express the things we don't like, because it has some immediate purpose in mind: to change the other people close to us in the hope of making ourselves feel better. In the intimacy of family, it is very easy to pin our problems on one another's actions. We thus feel the urgent need to point out each other's deficiencies and mistakes so that we can adjust our environment to be more the way we want it to be.

Appreciation is not utilitarian. It serves no immediate practical need: it does not get the kids out the door in time or the kitchen cleaned or phone messages delivered. Instead, it has a much deeper benefit to both the one appreciated and the one giving appreciation. With appreciation, relating becomes not just about getting things accomplished and needs met, but is a celebration of life meeting itself.

When we celebrate each other in a family, we support each other in blossoming fully into who we really are. Defenses relax. The family becomes our church, our temple, where we can feel the divine in each other and in our own hearts.

50

My Vision for Our Family

LEVEL OF DIFFICULTY ***

Sit together in a circle as a family,

Each person speaks a brief sentence starting with:

"My vision for our family is . . ."

When it is your turn, keep it to one basic theme or idea.

My vision for our family is:

That we have more time relaxing and doing nothing together.

That we go out more together and have fun.

That we buy a hot tub for the backyard.

Go around the circle until everyone in the family has spoken.

....

Any group of people thrives in an atmosphere of cocreation. When one person or group dominates over others, everyone loses: the dominated and the dominator are equally restricted by their roles.

The purpose of this practice is not so much to negotiate outcomes as it is to let everyone be heard and have the sense of being at the creative source of family life. Not everyone will get what they want, nor would that necessarily make them happy. But the structure of the family is shifted from a deaf hierarchy to an open space of freedom to express and listen.

We have used this practice often in our family; in the beginning, we would use it once a week, but it has gradually become less frequent, as the gestalt has changed. As the alpha male, I have learned to climb down from my pedestal of power and pay attention to the needs and visions of my loved ones. Through this practice, my two sons have realized that they have visions of their own and that there is the possibility of seeing their visions actualized. Hence their suggestions have become more realistic: they are no longer idle complaints but are real contributions to family life, which they know will be heard and have a decent chance of being acted upon.

It was through this practice that we decided together to turn off the lights more and use the money we saved for nicer food, to have quiet times together in the evening after dinner and keep movies to the weekend, and to do many projects around the house.

But more than any practical outcome, this practice broke down the imbalance of the adults (particularly the *man* of the house) making decisions and providing direction, and allowed us to relax into a deeper sense of community and Oneness.

51

Talk Gibberish

LEVEL OF DIFFICULTY ***

Whenever there is disagreement or disharmony in the family,
Or any time at all, just for the fun of it,
Switch to gibberish.
You will all continue to communicate
And connect fully with each other,
You will just stop making any sense.
Express everything that needs to be expressed inside you
Using nonsense words.
Keep going like this for a minimum of five minutes
Or for as long as fifteen minutes.
Have fun; be generous in your nonsense.
When you are done,
Keeping a straight face,
Try to remember what the problem was.

....

When we connect, there are always multiple dimensions occurring simultaneously in the interaction. All at once, our minds are trying to make sense of things, wanting to be right, pressing our own agenda, and defending against others. This is where we often get lost as a family, and are left feeling separate from our loved ones simply because we do not agree, often on an ultimately unimportant matter.

When you switch to gibberish, the logical dimension of connecting is transcended, but the energy still flows. Now the communication has no logical purpose; it is just a way of allowing energy to flow for its own sake. You will discover through this practice that this is, in fact, much more fun and nourishing communication, and even that you feel closer to people when the logical has been flushed away.

We have used this practice often in our family. We have a code word—when things get too serious or intense, someone just says: "Gibberish." Then we keep the conversation going, with just as much gusto as before, but now instead of being logical we are simply phorshemphashing troobalddee mosrhfung.

It might be disorienting, like it was just now, if a logical sentence and train of thought suddenly ghoopangs mooshfartoo foorgantoble. What happened? It breaks the continuity of the mind, and we find ourselves manbang nooshbarat forbantbit. But that is the point, to break the stranglehold of the mind.

Try it out. You may feel much goosberiestier and share a great deal more foongatsong together when you abandon being reasonable and dive wholeheartedly into morshfangtooble shangsorbetty.

Section Nine

Nature Practices

U<small>NTIL NOT VERY LONG AGO</small>, the idea of *being in nature* would have seemed absurd, because there was nothing other than nature. Nature just means the way the earth is when it has not been modified by the human mind and actions.

The outer environment mirrors our internal state. The complexity of urban life, with its fast movement and rapidly changing stimuli, demands that we make quick decisions and responses: it is a reflection of the unnatural state of the human mind. Nature, on the other hand, reflects the natural state of consciousness: the awakened state where we know ourselves to be whole, complete, and in Oneness. Just being in nature brings us back to who we truly are.

Nature is a doorway to spirit, but without the impositions of religion. Nature brings you back into spirit, but it has no dogma, nothing to believe in. It teaches without words, speaking to the body instead of the mind. Nature gracefully includes seeming opposites like creation and evolution without even pausing to consider any contradiction. Nature demands of us no rituals, and damns no disbelievers. It silently teaches us by example, never through sermons. Water shows us how to flow around things without any rigid hard edges. Stones teach us how to weather all kinds of challenges, and to lose our edges over time. The wind teaches us the possibilities of being everywhere and nowhere at once, and the earth teaches us the lessons of stability and unwavering presence.

As the practices in this section will show you, nature practices do not require any doing from us, as much as opening and receiving. They are the feminine way.

52

Sit in the Same Spot Every Day

LEVEL OF DIFFICULTY *

Find a place in nature
Where you can go every day.
If you live in a city,
It could be a park or even a flowerbed,
But if you live near a forest, like we do,
Step into the wild outdoors.
Sit in exactly the same spot every day,
Facing in the same direction,
And just be with things as they are.
Feel through your skin;
Listen carefully;
Watch and pay attention to the colors and shapes and
movement.
Be aware of the movement of the trees,
The sounds and activities of small animals and insects.
The boundaries where you end
And nature begins
Will dissolve.

....

At the core of modern humanity's suffering is the feeling of separation. We feel separated from each other in the ways we relate. We feel separated from the other members of our family. We feel separated from each other in our religious beliefs. We feel separated financially, racially, nationally. We feel separated from ourselves and from nature and from the divine.

Nature is not a way to experience Oneness; nature *is* One. There is no me and not-me in nature: everything is interconnected. When you return to the same place every day, you are returning to an ecosystem that is constantly in relationship with itself. The bark of the tree is home to the ants, who move in and out of the earth. They are eaten sometimes by the birds, whose song fills the space, and whose excrement returns to the soil. Everything is part of everything else. Nature is making love to itself, and eating itself, and excreting itself on itself all the time. Nature is incestuous, cannibalistic, and totally uncivilized.

When you start to sit in the same spot every day, you will at first feel like an outsider. You are bringing your civilized mind into nature, like an intellectual from New York City trying to fit in on a farm. You may sit awkwardly on the edge of a tree trunk, trying not to get dirty or be bitten by bugs. And just as you may feel cut off from nature, so nature may also not yet open to you. But just wait a little while. As you relax into this place, it will affect you, and you will affect it as well. You will become a part of the ecosystem. You will be accepted into the family. After a while, you may even experience the trees and the birds welcoming you home each day.

Your visits to this place will become a *deeksha*: an initiation into Oneness.

53

Open to the Vastness of the View

LEVEL OF DIFFICULTY *

While walking in nature
On a trail or in the forest,
When you come to an opening
Or a sudden drop opening to a vista,
Stop.
Let the vastness of the view pull you into itself
And dissolve you in itself.
At the same time, let the vastness of the view
Enter you completely
And become your inner landscape.
Let the suddenness of the opening
Happen both within and without.

....

There are many great mystics who have passed through radical awakening while being in nature. In William Wordsworth's long poem "The Prelude," his initiation into his own natural state of limitlessness is mirrored on every page by his experience of nature. The twentieth-century author Douglas Harding, who wrote the book *On Having No Head,* passed through a radical awakening while hiking in the Himalayas. He had no expectations; he was a major in the British army on leave, thirty-three years old, taking a walk in the mountains. Suddenly, the path opened up into a vast panorama, so he could see for miles around in every direction:

. . . a very still, clear day, and a view from the ridge where I stood over misty blue valleys to the highest mountain range in the world, made a setting worthy of the grandest vision. . . . It was all, quite literally, breathtaking. I seemed to stop breathing altogether, absorbed in the Given. Here it was, this superb scene, brightly shining in the clear air, alone and unsupported, mysteriously suspended in the void, and (and this was the real miracle, the wonder and delight) utterly free of "me," unstained by any observer. Its total presence was my total absence, body and soul. Lighter than air, clearer than glass, altogether released from myself, I was nowhere around.

There are many people who, like Douglas Harding, have had their heads removed by being in nature, by the vastness of the view. When you are out hiking, be open to nature as the great teacher, the great decapitator.

54

Stare into the Open Sky

LEVEL OF DIFFICULTY ***

Lie down on your back
Under a cloudless sky.
Open yourself to the nature of infinity.
Let yourself move out infinitely in any direction
And be soberly present with the unavoidable fact
That as far as you travel,
You are still only halfway there.
There are no limits.
You cannot *think* about infinity.
It will blow your mind.
You can only become one with the infinite.
Look into the sky without blinking.
Let the sky enter you, so there is no inner and outer remaining.
Then close your eyes and stare into the inner limitless sky.

....

This simple practice, to look into the open, cloudless sky, has been used in every tradition in every age. I was introduced to it in the Tibetan refugee community of Bodh Nath in Katmandhu by the great Dzogchen teacher Choki Nyima Rimpoche. Once it is pointed out to you, it becomes so obvious—it was there all along. Many of us get involved in spiritual practices and teachings, searching for who we really are, and the answer is right there above our heads all along: you only have to look up into the vastness of the sky. This practice is great for modern humanity, as we have grown so used to a man-made world. Everything has been modified; everything has our fingerprints all over it, except the sky. The vastness of the sky cannot be touched, cannot be modified; it remains the last outpost of absolute innocence.

The sky is such a great teacher, a great mirror, because it is not a thing. It is a presence. It contains all things, but it cannot be contained. Things have a beginning and an end in time, things have limits in space. But the sky has no creation date, it can never be destroyed, and it has no physical limits. There is a word for it, but there is no *thing* to which the word points, only spaciousness.

The sky can teach you about your own true nature. Consciousness is also not a thing. It also contains all of your experience, although it is not an experience. It, too, was never created, and has no limits. You also have a name, but if you follow that name back to where it points, you will find nothing there.

Imagine a vast empty space, extending equally in all directions. Now imagine a door in that space, without any wall around it, just a door in a door frame. There is space on one side of the door, and there is space on the other side of the door. Step through the door, and you step out of space and into space. How many spaces are there; how many infinities?

Staring into the sky is just like that. Look up into the sky, and there is infinite space. Look back into yourself, and there is infinite space. That which you call "me" is just a door in infinity, with infinite space behind it and before it and all around it. The infinite space of the sky and the infinite space of who you truly are are not two. "Space" is a word for Oneness.

55

Feel Nature Through Your Skin

LEVEL OF DIFFICULTY ***

Go out walking in nature.

It could be in the forest, or on the beach, or by a river.

If possible walk barefoot.

Let yourself feel the trees,

The dew,

The sun,

And the earth itself,

Through your skin.

Allow nature to be a sensuous experience.

Let yourself be caressed

By nature as a lover.

....

Nature is entirely feminine. Whether you are a man or a woman, whether you are straight or gay, she does not mind. She will seduce you anyway. Nature is shy, and won't reveal herself fully to you until she knows you come in sacredness; she has been raped by mankind for too long. If you respect her, if you visit her in the early morning when commerce is still asleep, or at night, or if you are willing to travel far into her interior, she will show you her secrets of sensual love.

You cannot have any connection with her through your mind. She never lives there; she cannot. She will sway and breathe and run from concepts. You cannot really know her very deeply through watching her or listening to her. That is a kind of voyeurism that she will tolerate, but with disinterest. She might pose pretty for you, offer you a nice vista here and there, but she will be relieved when you drive away again in search of other entertainment.

She will meet you only in the physical. That is her métier. Give her your naked feet, and she will open to you and reveal her gifts. When you see a moist and shadowy mossy place, throw your civilized habits to the winds and lie down on the moss. Touch her with your naked skin. Dive into her cool pools; be warmed by her boulders in the sun. Rub yourself against her bark. Then dance in the secret places of her forest and become One with her.

Nature is a lover. She will bring you home to yourself if you are willing to be washed clean of all that is not her.

56

Talk to Trees and Plants and Animals

LEVEL OF DIFFICULTY ****

When you walk alone in nature,
Stop to talk to trees and plants.
They are living beings, just like you.
They take their nourishment from the earth,
And they give back also.
Let a tree know that you mean it no harm,
That you come in peace.
When you see a deer or a squirrel
Be still, and talk quietly.
You can use words or communicate silently;
They will understand either one.
As you make friends with trees and plants and animals,
They will also make friends with you.

....

The way we communicate as human beings is very narrow. It is all channeled through the conceptual mind. When we talk to each other, we share thoughts about the past, about the future; we share concepts about things. We talk about anything except what we are actually experiencing now.

Because we are used to this very mental kind of communicating, we have lost the art of communicating with nonhuman life. There is plenty of it, all around us. Trees and plants and animals are all giving and receiving energy with each other, and with us, all the time. They just don't *think* in the way that we do. You can connect with them through speaking about what is real now, or just thinking it, or just feeling it. Tell a tree that it is beautiful, thank it for its shade and magnificence, be soft and receptive, and you will feel it reach back to you.

Let an animal, even your cat or your dog, feel that you are an animal also, that you also eat and sleep and like to touch and be touched. The insane idea of the hierarchy between you will dissolve, and you will feel Oneness.

Section Ten

Devotional Practices

THE GREAT SAGE RAMANA MAHARSHI lived and died in South India in the first part of the twentieth century. He was the inspiration to so many contemporary teachers, including my own teacher, H. W. L. Poonjaji. Ramana is best known for advocating the practice of self-inquiry, or *vichara*. He is renowned for saying that sincerely and deeply asking "Who am I?" is the only method needed for contemporary humanity. But he also taught another, seemingly contradictory approach: *bhakti*, or devotion.

Inquiry into the real nature of things and true devotion are seemingly opposite in their starting point, but they both bring you out of yourself and into Oneness. When you ask, "Who am I?" like we did in practice 7, you move deeper, through the layers of an imagined "me," until only space remains. The "me" has been seen through as an illusion, and what remains is reality. When you love deeply and beyond reason or logic, you also start to dissolve as a "me," and only the other remains. When the "me" has been lost completely, and only the beloved is there, this is devotion. Pure awakening and pure devotion come to the same thing: there is no me; there is no other; there is only the divine, only Oneness.

Fundamentalists will tell you that what is important is to be devoted to the one true deity, and that all others are false. And for that person it must be so. But for devotion to free you from the illusion of separation, it is only the purity of losing oneself in total devotion that matters. It will work no matter what face you give to the divine. So many great Christian saints have known God through total devotion to Jesus; the Indian sage Meera was washed clean of the illusion of separation through her love of Krishna; Rumi reached the peaks of absorption through his devotion to his teacher, Shaams.

Devotion starts with love. If that love takes more of a human and physical dimension, it becomes desire and relationship, and often can bind you more and more. If the same love takes on a dimension of the spirit, it becomes devotion, and it will free you of yourself more and more.

Love starts with the I and the other, the me and the not-me. As the love increases more and more, the I becomes less, and the other becomes more luminous. When the I dissolves completely, then there is also no other. That is Oneness.

57

Dance with the Divine

LEVEL OF DIFFICULTY ***

Close the door.

Switch off the ringer on the phone.

Lock the front door.

Leave the world behind for a while.

Put on your most beautiful clothes.

Put on some sacred music

That fills your heart with gladness

And reminds you of a gratitude that is not of this world.

As the music plays, let yourself dance with the divine.

Let yourself be danced *by* the divine.

Be taken over by the music,

And give yourself to the love that arises only out of silence,

Only where me and other have been left behind.

For a while, do this practice every night before you go to sleep.

Or, if you have friends who can meet you here,

Whom you can trust with your greatest tenderness,

You can do this practice together.

....

The great Persian mystic Rumi had his profound awakening with his teacher Shaams. He penetrated the deepest mystery, and came to know the place where the words "me" and "other" no longer had any meaning. But Rumi was above all a poet and a lover. He was not so interested in the truth of discrimination; he was interested in the truth of the heart. So he called out in his prayers, which also become his poetry, "I know that we are one. I know that there is no me and no you. But please, let there be just enough separation remaining that I can love you, be loved by you, be devoted to you." Such is the heart of the devotee.

This current of love between the devotee and the divine is called prayer. It is a strange thing, because the different religions of the world do not agree about who has the right deity, or the right theology, or the correct maps of heaven. In fact, they are willing to go to war over such differences. But in their means to reach out to the divine, they all converge. Prayer and devotion are universal language. Everyone prays; everyone bows in surrender and devotion.

Prayer can have so many dimensions. It can be a begging for more stuff, even for support in victory in violent wars. It can be a bowing in shame and an asking for forgiveness. It can be a calling out in gratitude. But for prayer to really speak the language of the divine more than of the human psyche, it needs to go beyond mind and thinking. This is where music and dance are such a miracle. When your communion with the divine involves your whole body, when you are taken over by the music and by the devotion, you no longer exist as a separate me, and you are transported into the world of God.

58

Feel Devotion to Those Close to You

LEVEL OF DIFFICULTY *****

Set aside a day
As an act of worship.
Rise early, wash, and put on clean clothes
As if you are preparing for a wedding.
If it is part of your life to pray or meditate,
This is a good day to connect before you leave the house.
See everyone and everything as a manifestation of the divine.
Look with the eyes of devotion.
There is no need to bow or scrape or *namaste*,
Or even to change your outward behavior in any way
To suggest to anyone that this day is different than any other.
This practice is a change of perception, not of behavior.
The effects will last for many days.
Do not do this practice very often
Or it will quickly become stale.

....

This is an advanced practice, and not one to start out with. To be
done properly, it requires sobriety and awareness of your shadow
sides and projections. You can start out with very small doses:
bring a quality of devotion to the person at the cash register in the
supermarket. Don't do it in any outward way, but simply in the
way that you perceive people and how you feel them in your heart.
Bring a quality of devotion to your child or your spouse, just for a

few minutes at a time. You can build up to longer periods of time, and a greater variety of people.

For many of us, the most difficult assignment, but also the most powerful, is to bring this practice into the workplace and be able to see our bosses and co-workers as deities. This is a very high level of practice. There is a taboo, especially in the Western world, that our place of work and feelings of love, devotion, and spiritual awakening have no common ground. But what a waste! Most people spend at least eight hours a day at work, and if you add in the time to get there and the time to get home, and the time spent preparing for work and the time spent unwinding, most of your life is work-related. If your connection with the divine is shut out of your work, what do you have left?

Everyone has had feelings of devotion from time to time. Perhaps when you have prayed, or when you have met a very great teacher or mystic, your heart has overflowed with devotion. It may have happened in a moment of great beauty, perhaps upon seeing a sunset or a magnificent work of art. We have the tendency to think that these feelings were caused by the teacher or the deity or the sunset, but they are also just symptomatic of an open and loving heart. As difficult as it sounds, there's no reason you can't bring this same openness to the people close to you in your day-to-day life.

59

Give Thanks for Blessings

LEVEL OF DIFFICULTY **

At the end of your day
Kneel down in gratitude
And give thanks for the blessings of the day.
Release all sense of accomplishment for now.
Let go of any entitlement.
It was all a gift.
Find a picture of one who represents the divine to you,
Or pictures of all those who do.
Give thanks for each and every thing.

....

We were all born into this world with empty hands, and one day we will all die in the same way. No matter how much power we may assume, how much wealth we may accumulate, or how many people we may persuade to support us, in the end we will all die in the same way: alone and empty-handed. You will most likely also suffer small deaths in your life along the way: bad investments, crushed expectations, the end of a marriage, the death of a loved one. In these deaths, you are shocked out of the feeling of entitlement so prevalent in our society, and into the recognition that everything has been borrowed; everything has been a gift.

Alexander the Great was a supremely powerful king and conqueror. At the age of thirty-two, he became very sick, and soon realized he would die. He called his generals to him, and told them that he had three last wishes. The first was that his doctor would carry his coffin alone. The second was that gold, silver, and gems should be scattered along the path where his coffin would be carried. And the third was that he should be buried with his hands outside the coffin. Only his closest general dared ask why. It is said that Alexander explained that these were the three lessons he had learned: that there is no physician who can save you from death when the time comes; that wealth ultimately means nothing to you; and, most important, that he came into this world with empty hands and so now he would also leave the world with his hands empty. He closed his eyes, fell silent, and died.

Giving thanks every night for blessings you have received releases that sense of entitlement. It reminds us that we are, essentially, always empty-handed. To live life in desire, no matter how much or how little you may have, is to live in lack. To live life in gratitude, no matter how rich or poor you may be, is to live in genuine abundance.

60

Surrender

LEVEL OF DIFFICULTY ***

At any time of the day
But especially when things are not going well,
Release control.
And hand it all over to the divine.
Just take your hands off the steering wheel.
When you made a reservation at a restaurant but find there is
no table for you,
You want to argue.
Instead, surrender.
Find another restaurant.
Surrender not with resignation,
But with trust:
The trust that the divine takes perfect care of you.

....

When my two sons were still quite small, I used to take them to the amusement park. There was a ride for very young children: a small train on a winding track, with a separate vehicle for each child. One vehicle was a duck, one was a small car, one was a steam engine, and one was a small airplane. Each vehicle was attached to the next, and each one had a steering wheel. The whole procession went extremely slowly. Despite the fact that they were following a track, each child would vigorously steer to the left or the right, like a race car driver. Occasionally, the train would actually go in the direction they were steering. Other times, they would be steering with great energy to the left as the whole procession was going to the right. Naturally, sometimes they would get upset and confused, but of course the whole thing was on a track—it didn't matter which way my young sons steered, or indeed if they steered at all. The train would go where it was destined to go, and that was that.

We put a great deal of our energy into trying to control the outcome of our life, steering this way or that with great energy. Sometimes, we have the insight that it makes very little difference. Our train, too, is on tracks; it is going where it is going. This insight is simply called surrender. At first we surrender cautiously, just a little bit at a time. Lo and behold, things go much better than we could ever have planned them. So we surrender some more, and with bigger things. And they go even better.

Something or someone is taking care of things, driving the train, with intelligence, grace, and humor. We do not know their e-mail address or cell number to thank them. But we can let go, trust, and enjoy the ride.

61

Couples Puja

LEVEL OF DIFFICULTY ****

When you wake in the morning,
Sit opposite each other on the bed.
Take turns doing this practice.
Look into one of your partner's eyes.
One of you will go first:
When it is your turn
Express love, devotion, and surrender to your partner.
See your beloved as the deity.
Tell your beloved of the depth of your commitment,
That your beloved knows you better than you know yourself.
Surrender to the guidance of the beloved.
Bow to your beloved; bring your head all the way to
the mattress;
Surrender yourself completely.
Then switch roles.

....

This is a powerful practice to do with your intimate partner. In
my life, I have been blessed to be close to some of the greatest
teachers of our time and to have received profound teachings and
tools that have helped me immensely. Furthermore, I have found
an extraordinary support group all over the world, an extended
sangha, a community of like-minded and openhearted friends. Supremely blessed as I have been, nothing and no one has come close

to bursting the bubble of illusory separation like my marriage to Chameli, my wife.

When you go to see a teacher, you are on your best behavior. You sit with a straight spine; you ask the right questions; you appear to be the model student. When you take as your guru your connection with your beloved, it is not like that at all. There is no time to prepare and nowhere to hide. In the morning, when I first open my eyes still drugged from sleep, there she is, in my face. "Are you here? Are you present? Can I count on you to show up and be present?"

When you take your marriage to be your guru, there is no time off. It is a serious commitment. If you are willing to open to your beloved as your guide, if you are willing to accept that your beloved knows your shadows and weaknesses better than you know them yourself, then you have surrendered to a strong medicine.

This requires commitment and a dedication of the relationship every day. We have done this simple practice every day for many years. It sets the tone of the day. It is a conscious choice to melt down defenses, again and again, and to intentionally see the divine in the eyes of your beloved. At first it may be difficult, and you may feel foolish or defensive: "Just last night she was making such a fuss about nothing, and today I have to bow down to her as a deity?" But bring that also to the *puja*. The word "puja" means a ritual of worship, the invocation of divine power. It will grow on you. Confess your resistance, express your vision, lay down your defenses, and something will awaken between you that is not personal at all, that is the meeting of the divine masculine and the divine feminine in both of you. Practice this every day for several weeks, and it will open a resource that you can return to easily during the day.

62

Call Out in Longing

LEVEL OF DIFFICULTY ***

On the beach or in the forest,
Or alone in your room,
Call out to the divine to reveal itself to you.
Use your real voice and lips
To call out in longing to know God directly.
You can raise your voice loud:
Plead, bargain, and demand.
Take one bold step toward the divine,
And the divine will take a hundred steps toward you.

....

God has no face and no form. There is only Godliness. It is the purity of longing in the devotee that gives a face and a voice to the divine. All of us carry so many concepts about the nature of the divine from our childhood. We may have learned that God is very far away and that we must earn his attention and blessings. We may have been taught that God is a very strict patriarch, that he has all kinds of rules and conditions, and that he will punish us if we do not conform.

Through practice, however, we learn that the divine reveals itself fully to the devotee according the way the devotee approaches the divine. If you are very afraid and meek, you may experience a face of God that is stern and unavailable. If you are very obedient and conforming, you may find a face for the divine that has many rules and regulations. If you are ashamed of yourself and have been conditioned to feel a lot of guilt, you may experience the divine as punishing and unforgiving. You can create any relationship you want with the divine, and the divine will cooperate with you. Godliness can reveal itself as masculine or feminine, as old or young. God can be the divine mother; God can be your friend. Create the kind of relationship with the divine that allows you to feel divine love and support.

Call out in longing to the divine to reveal itself in a personal way. Call out as a child might call out to a mother or a father. Demand that you be heard. If you open yourself in a very personal and intimate way to the divine, then the divine will open to you in this way as well.

Compassion Practices

COMPASSION MEANS TO FEEL *WITH* the other, not to feel *for* the other. There are many practices that we can explore that can open our hearts to compassion. Compassion is not a means to an end. The perfume of compassion is awakening.

The word "compassion" comes from the Latin roots, *com* (with) and *pati* (to feel). When you feel with someone, there is no sense of hierarchy, no sense of looking down on someone. There is no gloating. The word "compassion" is so often used to mean "feel sorry for." "He's such a loser, I feel compassion for him; those poor people in Darfur, I feel compassion for them, too." This kind of compassion, well-meaning as it may be, still maintains the feeling of a me and a not-me. "I am warm and well fed; I have enough money and a loving family; I feel bad about the bum on the street; how can I help him out?" Even in this desire to help, his pain and failure are *his,* and my good fortune is *mine,* and between them lies a chasm of difference. Maybe I will toss a quarter across the chasm now and then, or maybe even help out in bigger ways, to ease my troubled conscience.

The kind of compassion we are pointing to in this section is quite different. Rather than a fortunate me helping out a less fortunate not-me, the compassion we're pointing to goes beyond the me and the not-me as separate. The pain and failure and despair that the bum on the street feels is also mine. The story may be a little different, but the roles could be so easily reversed. And what he feels, I can also feel. My good fortune is also his.

This kind of compassion is not a change of behavior, but an awakening to a deeper dimension. When we feel the other as ourselves, and see ourselves in the other, we are no longer compensating for the injustices of this world: we have shifted into a state of consciousness where the very roots of injustice can no longer flourish.

63

Just Like Me

LEVEL OF DIFFICULTY ***

Whenever a judgment or evaluation
Arises within you,
Whether positive or negative,
Add the three words: ". . . just like me."
You can go ahead and judge another as lazy,
But be inclusive with it:
He is so lazy, just like me.
She is arrogant, just like me.
They are incompetent,
She is unreliable,
He is angry,
Just like me.
Call back positive judgments in the same way:
The Dalai Lama is so wise, just like me.
She is so compassionate,
He is so strong,
Just like me.
In this way, call back every judgment to yourself
And realize that there is no other out there:
It is all you.

....

Why should it be that when you go to a gathering of people there is
always one person who irritates you completely, while your friends

or partner find that person quite interesting? And why should it be that someone whom your partner could not stand, you had no issue with? People are not bad or irritating in and of themselves. It is because we project our own disowned fragmented parts outside ourselves that we feel judgment.

It is the habit of the mind in separation to want to externalize everything. If we have not fully accepted the anger or hurt or rigidity we carry within our own hearts, we seek it out in others and blame or judge the qualities we see. You can walk into a room filled with a hundred people, and something unconscious will scan the room and cast out a lasso to the one person there who can reflect back to you the things you could not see or be with in any other way. Usually, we leave that quality out there in the crowd, projecting our disowned ghosts onto other people and situations. We judge another as lazy or rigid or cold or closed only when we do not want to see those tendencies in ourselves. It is in this way that we create division between a you and a me, an us and a them. On the other hand, if we can feel the judgment and immediately call it back, we can turn it into an opportunity to pass through a small process of expansion and growth.

These three simple words, "just like me," will transform judgment from separation to self-acceptance. Practice this as often as you can. You can use this practice silently inside yourself, or you can speak it out loud. Either way, you will start to laugh at what previously seemed so serious and begin to celebrate the areas of yourself that had been hidden by your judgments.

64

The Heart Meditation

LEVEL OF DIFFICULTY ***

Sit comfortably with your spine straight and your chest open.

Bring your attention to the middle of your chest.

Imagine the heart center to be a window

Into the vastness that is your true nature.

Now, with the in-breath, absorb whatever is before you:

Objects, sounds, thoughts, and feelings.

Bring them all home into formlessness

So that they dissolve into silence, into space.

With the out-breath,

Breathe a wave of blessing

Out of the formlessness,

Back into the world of form.

Continue in this way with your own experience:

With the in-breath embracing everything that arises

And welcoming it home into its source,

With the out-breath sending out waves of blessing.

Once this becomes natural and effortless,

Let it expand

To include the thoughts and feelings of those around you,

Also equally embraced home into emptiness

And also all equally blessed.

Finally, let this practice expand to include

All thoughts and feelings of all sentient beings.

....

This simple practice is based on the ancient Tibetan practice of Tonglen, which is used to this day in the traditions of Tibetan Buddhism to cultivate compassion. Besides being a very effective way to open the heart and become more compassionate, Tonglen also brings us quickly into Oneness, because it dissolves the separation of a me and a not-me. Although the practice predates him, Tonglen is most clearly elucidated by the Tibetan heart master Atisha, who lived in the eleventh century.

It is important always to start this practice with yourself, with your own thoughts and feelings, before you try to expand it to absorb and bless others as well. It will quickly become natural to you, because this is happening all the time anyway, only it is usually unconscious. You are simply bringing attention to it. By using the practice for thirty to forty minutes every day, the sense of "my thoughts" and "his thoughts" or "her thoughts" starts to dissolve: there are just thoughts, there is only one mind, it is everywhere, and we are all small receivers tuning into it, like radios. The sense of his jealousy, or her anger, or your pain, or my compassion, melts away: all of these feelings are collective.

This practice does not necessarily change the content of your experience, but it does slowly relax the habit to resist your experience just as it is, and gradually dissolves the sense of a me and a not-me.

65

Loving-Kindness

LEVEL OF DIFFICULTY **

Remember someone who has been very kind to you,
Who has shown you love and concern and embrace.
Feel the gift of that love in your heart.
Allow yourself, for a few moments, to feel that same kindness,
That same love and concern and embrace
For yourself.
Think of someone very close to you, and send that person
This same kindness, love, concern, and embrace.
Expand this same feeling to your parents, then to your family.
Expand it to all your good friends; shower them with
loving-kindness,
With this same love and concern for their well-being.
Send this same loving-kindness to everyone who is a part of
your daily life:
Your co-workers, your neighbors, the postman,
And the person who sells you groceries.
Now think of someone whom you do not like,
Who has wronged you in some way,
And send the same loving-kindness to this person as well.
Finally, expand the wave of loving-kindness to all
sentient beings.
Feel your concern for their well-being,
Send your embrace.

....

This simple practice was taught by the Buddha 2,500 years ago, and has been practiced by Buddhists all over the world ever since. It is the practice of cultivating what is known as *metta*, or loving-kindness. Of course, 500 years later this became the essence of the master Jesus's teachings: to love your enemy as yourself.

Loving-kindness is not only a moral virtue, or a way to make the world a better place; it is also a powerful practice to relax more deeply into Oneness. Loving-kindness is not something to be practiced or added to you: it is the essence of who you are. Anger, jealousy, control, and sadness: these are emotions that come and go. Loving-kindness is what remains when all of these emotions have been left behind. Through the conscious practice of loving-kindness, even for a few minutes a day, the seeds of separation between a sense of a me and a not-me dissolve, and we feel all sentient beings as our family.

People who have used this practice repeatedly over a few weeks report that they sleep better and wake feeling more refreshed. They get along better with everyone, both other human beings and even animals. Things go more easily, as if one is protected by an invisible force. Of course, if we are not holding harmful thoughts toward one another, we do not experience such thoughts being mirrored back to us by the outer world. Through the practice of loving-kindness, the mind becomes more clear and sharp, and meditative states become spontaneously deeper and more abiding.

66

Radical Forgiveness

LEVEL OF DIFFICULTY ****

You can use this practice when you feel someone
has wronged you,
Or you can use it when remembering some past hurt.
Whenever you feel wounded, humiliated, or angry,
Hold the other as faultless.
Close your eyes for a few minutes and feel the hurt.
Breathe into this feeling, welcome it, and enjoy it.
The key here is to choose it as though from a menu,
To trust and know that this is old hurt.
It has been stored in the body,
And now it is being released.
Have strong intention to feel all of it,
To feel it to the very bottom
Until there is no more.
When it is no longer possible to find any more hurt
Breathe deeply—open your eyes
And give thanks to the one who gave you this gift.

....

Needless to say, this practice should be pursued with intelligence
and caution. If someone is really abusing you or taking advantage
of you, it may be more appropriate to take yourself out of harm's
way than to practice radical forgiveness. For this reason, always do
this practice with the support and encouragement of a group of

supportive friends, which you will find in practice 68, "Real Support," in the next section.

So what is the benefit of this practice? Forgiveness is not just a moral virtue that we practice to be a good person and to earn brownie points in heaven. Forgiveness is also the natural and effortless result of being willing to feel our feelings completely. You actually cannot really decide to forgive someone in any other way. If someone wrongs you, and the pain of that perceived wrongdoing is still held in the body, no matter how hard you try to practice the moral virtues of forgiveness, sooner or later that unmet pain will still surface and cause you to seek revenge, cut yourself off, or behave with "passive aggression," all the while with a sweet smile. There is nothing you can do about it, because the power of unconscious feeling is always much stronger than the decisions we make in the conscious mind.

The only real forgiveness is that which arises spontaneously from the willingness to feel without limits. And we choose that not as a moral virtue, but because we value freedom over limitation. The past is not healed; it simply ceases to be interesting. Our loyalty shifts from who did what to whom in the past to the vibrant mystery of this present moment.

67

Release All Blame

LEVEL OF DIFFICULTY *****

When you feel impatient, inconvenienced,
Or hurt in some way,
Seek to experience the limitations in which the other is living.
You will do this through your body and your feelings
More than through thinking.
If your boss is hard on you or puts you under pressure,
If your mother-in-law is critical,
Or even if a political leader seems to be insane,
Seek to feel their limitations in your own body.
Close your eyes, and invite yourself to feel
The tensions in your body that the other feels in theirs.
Feel the feelings that they feel,
And feel the ways they cannot feel.
Feel the rigidity of their beliefs
And the limits of their trust.
Feel the triumphs and failures of the one you have blamed.
Feel their hopes and fears.
In the willingness to feel all of this
Will arise the realization that this other person
Is doing the very best they can
Within the boundaries of their own private confinement.
In this insight
All blame is released.

....

This is an advanced practice, which should only be done with the support and encouragement of others who care about you.

There are many times in our lives when we need to stand up for ourselves, call out in righteous indignation when we feel stepped on, and take no more.

But an encrusted habit of blame leads to a pervading disposition of bitterness and eats at the soul. We are all interconnected. It is much easier than you might think to feel the pain of another. You absolutely know it is possible when it is someone very close to you. If your child falls and scrapes a knee, you feel it, too. When your beloved is sad or disappointed, you feel it, too. We only do not feel what another feels when we have "othered" that person far enough away that we have persuaded ourselves that their feelings and thoughts and bodily sensations belong to a different universe than our own. You can actually feel anything that anyone is feeling anywhere, and you can have the experience of anyone anywhere. The limit is not that we cannot feel with another but that we deeply do not want to open that much.

Blame is released from our reality when we see that there are no perpetrators anywhere, that we are all victims of a collective virus of separation. Just as if someone close to you had the flu and sneezed, and later you got sick: you might hold blame for a short time, but your deeper heart would let you know that you now have both been smitten by the same affliction.

We are all caught in a web of hurt—it is not personal. No one means you any harm, and no one ever has. The way out of the web is to hold everyone blameless, to feel their higher intention despite the surface appearance.

This is a very challenging practice to master. If you do, it will lead to a freedom beyond your capacity to imagine.

Section Twelve

Community Practices

IT MAY APPEAR THAT THE practices in this book and the shifts they precipitate are all about you and me, your state and my state. But as the awakening deepens, there is less and less interest in *me* at all, less interest in *my* problems, and less interest in *my* enlightenment as well. There comes the recognition that these are not *my* thoughts—they are all part of the collective mind; they belong to all of humanity. Pain is *our* pain; resistance is *our* resistance. And, too, the liberation that the heart calls for is *our* liberation. There cannot be full liberation in any one mind until there is liberation in the collective, because just below the surface appearance they are one and the same. For a wave in the ocean to become warmer, the whole ocean must become warmer; the waves are the same. One little wave might aspire to become tropically cozy, but if it is dancing in the middle of the Atlantic in December, it's not going to happen. None of us can drift very far from the collective consciousness in which we dance, of which we are made. In this realization, aspirations for and claims of enlightenment dissipate into simply being in service of all sentient beings, of Oneness—for that is what we all really are. The quantum shift of which we are all a part, and for which all translucent practice is a catalyst, is one that includes and carries all of us as One.

These few practices invite you to step out of the box in which you are used to living. They invite you into a generosity of spirit that is uncommon in our society but refreshing to the spirit. Rest assured, I have used these practices with groups all over the United States and Europe, and, radical as they are, so far they've gotten no one arrested! Be conscious and respectful of everyone around you so that your practice serves the opening and delight of everyone involved.

68

Real Support

LEVEL OF DIFFICULTY **

Meet on a regular basis with a group of friends who care about you,

And who care as much as you do about living translucently.

Make a commitment to support each other

In leaping out of the confines of old habit.

We all have arenas where we are already transparent and flowing,

Where the divine gushes through us free of restriction.

And we all have arenas of opacity,

Where we block the flow.

Be a support to each other.

Each person will have five to ten minutes to ask for support

In living more translucently.

That person will share where they feel blocked and restricted.

Then the whole group will decide—by unanimous consent—

On a practice or several practices from this book

That person will do regularly until the next meeting.

Everyone must agree, including the one who is to do the practice.

Everyone should have a turn in the hot seat.

....

Choosing the right practice is a very delicate art. You can go to a teacher, but odds are that the better and deeper a teacher is, the more he or she will be in demand, and the less time there will be to focus on your needs. You can try to self-prescribe practices, but often you are the last person on the planet you should be asking for advice. Why? Because we tend to choose out of our existing imbalance. A shy and retiring person will most likely read this book and feel attracted to the practices in the insight and meditation sections, practices that are easy to do alone, and so become even more imbalanced. A heady and intellectual person (. . . just like me) will likely revel in the insight section, but skip over the body practices altogether, and so become more imbalanced. An outgoing and gregarious party-animal will love this section on community, or the practices involving other people, but stay clear of meditation, and so possibly avoid going inside him or herself even more.

Vietnamese Zen teacher Thich Nhat Hanh said recently, "These days, the sangha [spiritual community] is the Buddha." Many other people share this view: that the enlightened messiah who has come to save humanity today is not a person but a collective awakening—the most reliable teacher is friends meeting friends. When you find a group of friends who care about the truth, who care about each other, and who share a similar depth of maturity and humor about themselves and each other, you have found your sangha. Value it deeply; it is the boat that will carry you safely across the swamps of imagined separation. Give yourself completely to such a gathering, and follow faithfully the guidance that it offers in consensus. This will be the best way to get value from this book.

69

Be an Invisible Angel

LEVEL OF DIFFICULTY **

Find small things you can do for other people
Anonymously.
Do this for people you know
As well as total strangers.
When it is the day to take out the trash
Carry someone else's to the road
Without them even knowing.
Find a dirty car, and wash it.
Leave chocolate in unexpected places.
Leave flowers, but take no credit.
Send notes of appreciation to people who are doing their best.
Take no credit,
But after some time, stop.
Check in and feel your inner landscape.

....

This practice is an art form: you are making more beauty with your life, as an end in itself. This kind of generosity of spirit hinges on the fact that no one ever knows that it was you. If you do this practice in any other way, it becomes a kind of moral virtue, a way to earn brownie points and elevate your status in the neighborhood or community. If it is used like that, it becomes a way of asserting moral superiority and can actually cause other people to feel worse about themselves. So you need to be very sure that these acts are done in a way that cannot be traced back to you.

On the other hand, you also need to be sure that these small anonymous gifts are really wanted and will be valued. Do not impose your values on another person. Make sure that they would like to get home and find the lawn mowed before you get busy. If you want to repaint an old lady's fence while she is at the doctor's office, be sure that the color is one she likes. If there is any doubt, you risk causing irritation rather than delight, and further still, you risk getting arrested.

Do not feel concerned; in just a few minutes you, will come up with at least a dozen such acts of generosity that are guaranteed to delight and cause no offense. Small gifts, money put in the pocket of someone who needs it, anonymous notes of appreciation, flowers, chocolates, cleaning: there is plenty of room for acts of random kindness in this world.

You are the world; the world is you. The fascination with *my* well-being, my success, my happiness, and ultimately my spiritual state is counterproductive. The heart's deepest longing is satisfied when we transcend the me and its small needs. This practice will shift your attention from me to us.

70

Compliment Three Strangers

LEVEL OF DIFFICULTY ****

This practice is best done with a friend.

One will do the practice,

And one will act as a witness and support

At a distance.

Go into a place where there are people you do not know:

A shopping mall, restaurant, bank, or park.

Compliment three people you have never met.

I love your nail polish.

Thank you for the radiant presence you bring to your job.

You have beautiful eyes.

Approach an old couple

And tell them how much love you can feel between them.

See how far you can step out on a limb

In spreading into this world a little more irrational generosity.

Do not upset anyone, but equally do not hold back.

Step beyond the habitual limits of socially acceptable restraint.

....

From time to time, I teach in corporations, even at Harvard Law School. I hope that I am able to serve corporate America in some small way, because the CEOs, CFOs, and attorneys who attend those seminars certainly serve me in helping me letting go of arrogant prejudice. You see, I had previously assumed that if you wanted to find people sincerely interested in living in a deeper way, in reaching out to the divine and bringing love down into daily life, you would need to look among psychologists, writers, maybe social workers or schoolteachers. But lawyers and executives? Nah. They just care about money and power.

I have included this exercise, and many others like it, in every corporate training I have conducted. I have let executives loose on downtown areas to compliment strangers, to give other people shoulder massages who are in line at a fast-food restaurant (with no explanation provided), to carry groceries for old ladies. I had two unexpected revelations with these mad experiments. The first was how willing corporate America was to make a fool of itself— to take a walk on the wild side. The second was how deeply and quickly these people were transformed by such a simple practice.

Stepping out of the box in this way gives us permission to unleash a tidal wave of generosity and longing to connect that has been locked up behind decades of concepts about what is permissible.

Try this practice. It is exciting, energizing, and often will yield stories you can tell your grandchildren when you are old.

71

Make Yourself into Live Entertainment

LEVEL OF DIFFICULTY *****

This is a practice to do with a group of friends.
If you form a practice group (described in practice 68),
It would be ideal to do together as a group.
Go to a public place together,
Like a restaurant, bar, or park.
Decide on a practice for one person at a time
(Which everyone must agree on, including the one doing it)
That will provide energy and entertainment
To the community at large.
One person might have the task to sing in a restaurant,
One might play with the children in a park,
One might do impersonations, or juggle.
Make sure that each assignment serves everyone involved:
The one doing the assignment, and everyone effected by it
(With no exceptions).
Ensure that everyone in your group has a turn.

....

The natural state of a human consciousness is to feel Oneness. The Swiss developmental psychologist Jean Piaget demonstrated that small babies do not perceive any boundary between where they end and the outside environment begins. A baby holds a toy and immediately feels at one with it. A baby looks at the mother and merges completely. There is no sense of a separate self. An awakened sage has the same experience of reality: no separate me, only that which is seen and that which is heard, with no one hearing and no one seeing. The essence of the disease of the human condition is the feeling of a me and a not-me.

This simple practice is a powerful and challenging way to step out of yourself. This is not a gentle nudge; this is a dramatic leap beyond the comfort zone. For this reason, it would be almost impossible to do alone, without the support of a group.

Do not announce to people that you have an assignment or that you are doing a practice from some crazy book you found. Don't pass the responsibility on to me! You will have to stand on your own feet here. Together with your support group, you will need to decide on the right balance of stretch and comfort. If you stretch too much, you will just close down in fear and traumatize yourself. If you do not stretch enough, it will be too easy, and it will not serve you. With the right degree of stretch, you feel energized, excited, and challenged, but you have fun with it. And the ultimate litmus test of this practice is that you shift the people around you, in the restaurant or the park or the mall, into greater aliveness, connection, and energy. If you can get people to participate with you, by singing, dancing, hugging, or in any other way, you have made the world a more expansive place.

72

Give Love Now

LEVEL OF DIFFICULTY ***

In the midst of conflict,
When you feel separate, distant,
Stop.
Close your eyes if you need to,
And drop inside yourself.
Find your own way to rediscover your commitment to love,
To feel the ocean of what is deeper and more abiding
Underneath the waves of passing moods.
If these were to be your last few minutes on this earth
What would be really important?
Take a breath.
Reconnect.
Leap before you look.
Give love now,
Totally.

....

Why? Find one good reason why on earth not.

Acknowledgments

I HAVE BEEN BLESSED WITH SOME wonderful teachers and wise friends in my life, and all of the practices in this book are, in one way or another, gifts to me from someone else. It is all recycled.

Some of the extraordinary people who have influenced the creation of this book (in no particular order) are Ramana Maharshi, H. W. L. Poonjaji, Osho (Bhagavan Shree Rajneesh), Urgyen Tulku Rimpoche, Chyoki Nyima Rimpoche, Robert Dickinson, Chameli Ardagh, Gay and Kathlyn Hendricks, Lester Levenson, Hale Dwoskin, Byron Katie, David Frawley, Christian Opitz, Sofia Diaz, David Deida, Saniel Bonder, Mantak Chia, Margot Anand, Douglas Harding, Sri Bhagavan and Sri Amma of the Oneness University, Jack Kornfield, Barbara Marx Hubbard, Carolyn Anderson, John Zwerver, and Brad Blanton.

Thanks to the wonderful and patient people at Sounds True: Tami Simon, Kelly Notaras, Tara Lupo, Chantal Pierrat, Haven Iverson, Dean Olson, and Elisabeth Rinaldi—and to my outside editor, Andrew Merz.

And, as always, many thanks to my family. My wife, Chameli, has been my practice partner for many years now, and each and every one of the practices in this book has been tried and tested within the crucible of our sacred marriage. My sons, Abhi and

Shuba, are my Zen teachers as well as my beloveds and my inspiration for a saner world. Garrett Stanley, our manager, has become a member of our family, and his attention to detail has allowed me to have the space in my life to write this book and to do many other fun things.

Appendix: Going Deeper

ONCE YOU HAVE DIGESTED THE practices in this book, you might like to go deeper.

Feel free to contact us.

Arjuna Ardagh sometimes is available for private sessions, by telephone or in person, to help you find the right practices for your life.

Arjuna travels and teaches frequently in the United States and in Europe. See our website for the schedule. If you would like to invite Arjuna to speak and to conduct a weekend workshop in your church or community, please e-mail us.

We also offer teleconferences over the phone and Internet. Details are available on the website.

If you are able to organize a small group with whom to practice on a regular basis, you can invite Arjuna to work with your group on a regular basis, by conference call or even in person.

We also offer a training, for those who work with people professionally, to become a spiritual counselor. The full 600-hour training leads to certification and ordination as a minister with the Living Essence Foundation.

For more information:

Living Essence Foundation
www.livingessence.com
1-888-VASTNES (1-888-827-8637)
godeeper@livingessence.com

About the Author

ARJUNA ARDAGH IS THE FOUNDER of the Living Essence Foundation in Nevada City, California, a nonprofit church dedicated to the awakening of consciousness within the context of ordinary life. He is the author of *Awakening into Oneness, The Translucent Revolution, Relaxing into Clear Seeing, How about Now?*, and *The Last Laugh* (a novel). He is the host of the *Awakening into Oneness* DVD series. He is the creator of *Let Yourself Go*, a six-CD audio set, the *Living Essence Audio Series, Living Essence Live*, and many other audio and video products.

Ardagh was educated in England, at Kings School, Canterbury, and later at Cambridge University, where he earned a master's degree in literature. Since the age of fourteen, he has had a passionate interest in spiritual awakening, and he began to practice mediation and yoga at that time. In his late teens, he trained as a meditation teacher. After graduating from Cambridge, Ardagh devoted himself completely to the call he felt inside, and studied and lived with a number of great spiritual teachers, both in Asia and in the United States. In 1987, he founded the Alchemy Institute in Seattle, Washington.

In 1991, he returned to India for a period of prolonged meditation and met H. W. L. Poonjaji, a direct devotee of the great sage Ramana Maharshi, with whom he went through a radical awakening. After returning to the United States, he began to share this awakened view with other people at Poonjaji's request, facilitating a dramatic shift in awareness with thousands of people throughout the United States and Europe. In 1995, Ardagh developed the Living Essence Training, which prepares people to be facilitators of this shift in consciousness and to cultivate translucence.

Ardagh was invited to the Oneness University in the winter of 2005, and he now integrates the Oneness Blessing (Deeksha) into all of the other work he does. He speaks at many international conferences, and has appeared on TV, on the radio, and in print media in twelve countries. He also teaches the Deeper Love seminars with his Norwegian wife, Chameli Gad Ardagh. They live in Nevada City with his two sons. You may contact him at:

arjunaa@livingessence.com

www.livingessence.com

About Sounds True

....

SOUNDS TRUE WAS FOUNDED IN 1985 with a clear vision: to disseminate spiritual wisdom. Located in Boulder, Colorado, Sounds True publishes teaching programs that are designed to educate, uplift, and inspire. With more than six hundred titles available, we work with many of the leading spiritual teachers, thinkers, healers, and visionary artists of our time.

To receive a free catalog of wisdom teachings for the inner life, please visit www.soundstrue.com, call toll-free 800-333-9185, or write: The Sounds True Catalog, P.O. Box 8010, Boulder CO 80306.